THE THING ABOUT FOOTBALL

THE SONGS OF GREG CHAMPION

The Slattery Media Group Pty Ltd

Level 39/385 Bourke Street, Melbourne

Victoria, Australia, 3000

Text © Greg Champion [BMG Publishing]
© Greg Champion

Design © The Slattery Media Group Pty Ltd, 2018

Published by The Slattery Media Group, 2018

All rights reserved. No part of this publication may be reproduced, stored in a retrieval system or transmitted in any form or by any means without the prior written permission of the copyright owner. Inquiries should be made to the publisher. Inquiries should be made to the publisher.

 A catalogue record for this book is available from the National Library of Australia

Group Publisher and editor: Geoff Slattery
Design: Kate Slattery
Typeset: Stephen Lording
Illustrations: Colin Suggett

Printed in Australia by Griffin Press

slatterymedia.com

THE THING ABOUT FOOTBALL

THE SONGS OF
GREG CHAMPION

I've got my scarf got my old coat
I've got a footy game to go to
Footy's on, footy's here again
Back to greet me like an old friend, and

That's the thing about
That's what I like about
That's the thing about, the thing about
football, woh-oh

visit *slatterymedia.com*

Well I went out to have a bat just the other day.
I had no conception what was coming my way,
I played a chanceless innings
& I made a 100 in the backyard at mum's
earnt every run

Oh I made a hundred in...
I clobbered & I crunched every fabulous run
I toiled & I sweated & when the day was done
I'd made a 100~...

I started out real shaky just prodding around
My sister with her off breaks
she had me tied down
But when me little brother bowled
& when we stopped for lunch I was
I ane tying the door

There me Uncle Nev—...
But I was scoring freely with
reflections
As I passed my 50 I paused for
& when I hit the roof next door
they all

Where it all began: Draft of 'I made a hundred in the backyard at mum's'

Contents

FOREWORD

**06 Taking the Mickey (TTM)...
in the nicest possible way (NPW)**

By Ian Cover

INTRODUCTION

09 A ditty a day

By Greg Champion

13 THE 1980s

It all begins with a few songs for a laugh in Adelaide,
then comes *The Coodabeen Champions*.

41 THE 1990s

The Coodabeens go national, then commercial, and
That's What I Like About Football becomes a theme for the AFL game.

65 THE 2000s

Back to the ABC and more songs on the radio.

95 THE 2010s

A new producer joins the crew,
and *The Coodabeens* grow old, gracefully...

145 AND ALSO

There's more to life on the road than footy songs
and ditties; and then there are poems...

FOREWORD

Taking the Mickey (TTM) ... in the nicest possible way (NPW)

By Ian Cover

It's half a lifetime ago now but I'll never forget when old school mate Billy Baxter rang to suggest we should check out a band from South Australia that was new on the Melbourne pub scene. And so off we went to see *The Fabulaires* featuring a lanky guitarist-singer who was front and centre of the line-up. His name was Greg Champion.

We were fascinated by Champs' cheerful demeanour and his happy banter with the crowd in between leading the band through a string of up tempo songs which kept the dance floor packed. We were also enthralled by the way he rotated his way through a range of colourful sunglasses and then there was his show-stopping leap into the audience from atop the PA stack while pumping out a lively guitar riff.

Almost 40 years later, we're still in Greg's musical thrall as he straps on his guitar and plys his trade on our Saturday morning ABC Radio footy show as a member of *The Coodabeen Champions*. He doesn't wear the sunnies any more—it wouldn't work on radio, of course—and there's no jumping off the studio desk to end his song segment.

But the songs have kept coming. Thousands, yes, thousands of them since 1983. Hundreds written by Greg and hundreds contributed by listeners; and then hundreds more by a combination of Greg and the listeners including his growing stable of long-time collaborators. Together, they have produced a staggering output and made a remarkable contribution to the show and to the culture of footy.

Players, teams, games, grounds, fans, uniforms, umpires, rules, incidents, controversies, brouhahas, you name it—just about anything and everything that has happened in the past four decades of footy has been the subject of a Champs ditty. Sometimes, the lyrics trail off and Greg's mouth trumpet or a *roody-doody-do* kicks in but we get the idea.

Oddly enough, Greg's first foray into waxing lyrical about footy on radio was *sans* music. He had written some poems about the game and Billy Baxter, having met Champs through our ventures to pub venues, invited him to read them on Billy's program on 3RRR on Thursday mornings. In turn, Billy invited Greg to do it again on *The Coodabeens'* Saturday footy show, then in its early days.

This led to some bright spark suggesting that Greg set the words to music. An early contributor to the show came up with *(The Answer My Friend Is Like) Kicking Into The Wind* to Bob Dylan's *Blowin' In the Wind*. Mike Brady had created the footy anthem *Up There Cazaly* in 1979, but this was a whole new take on footy songs. And it worked on two levels: firstly, the lyrics gently poked fun at the subjects and, secondly, often took the Mickey out the songs and tunes that were the basis for the parody.

Things really started moving when Greg recorded *(I'm) Dipierdomenico* at 3AW one Friday morning in 1986. A producer grabbed the tape and took it around to the studio where Derryn Hinch was presenting his top-rating morning program. Within minutes, the *Dipper* song was on the airwaves and the switchboard lit up with requests for a replay.

Channel Seven jumped on it and produced a video clip featuring Dipper in action and screened it on *World Of Sport*. At *The Coodabeens*, we like to think we set the Hawk wingman on the road to Brownlow glory later that year. Dipper, on the other hand, claims he made us!

Whichever way you look at it, this mainstream exposure for Greg's work put him on the road to an association with Channel Seven that later saw *Red Hot Go* and *The Thing About Football* both being used as themes for their footy coverage. It was—and remains—a huge buzz for all of us that those songs have provided a soundtrack to the football lives of generations.

The songs also were instrumental in getting us onto the MCG on Grand Final day in 1987 as part of the half-time entertainment, and again pre-match in 1995. We landed the 1995 spot after "passing the audition" with a pre-match spot before the State of Origin game when Ted Whitten made his emotional farewell to football. Greg penned the song *Don't Let The Big V Down* which we performed minutes before Ted entered the arena for one last lap of the ground.

That was unforgettable; as was the day a couple of years earlier when Ted asked Greg to record a version of the North Melbourne theme song for the Victorian team, substituting Victoria for North Melbourne in the lyrics. Ted joined us in the studio, donned the headphones and joined in the chorus with enormous gusto. You can hear him adding "hey" at the end of just about every line. Greg thought about trying to get Ted to exercise some control but sensibly gave up.

The singalong approach has evolved in the radio studio and onto live shows we perform from time to time. We love it and so do the listeners and concert audiences. Everyone has a favourite song and even the players who have been targeted have seen the funny side. Of course, in *Coodabeens* speak, the songs and their sentiments are always meant in the NPW (Nicest Possible Way).

David Rhys-Jones received the double whammy from Champs, being hailed both in poem and song, and gave his approval. Dermott Brereton copped his serve in *Dermott Brereton Is A Hood* and loved it, but his mum was not too pleased.

And, as for stereotyping, Melbourne fans are forever linked to the snow, a point Greg even sends himself up in *Members Of The MCC* when he sings *"I'm tired of all these jokers singing sarcastic songs about the Dees."* The Collingwood songs keep coming, too, with *The Train To Montmorency* brilliantly summing up Pies fans.

The lyrics to this classic and more than 100 others are published here (along with a swag of his non-footy songs) as a record and an acknowledgement of the combined creative skills of Greg Champion and all the contributors to this vital part of *The Coodabeen Champions'* radio show.

Above all, they're here for your enjoyment so TTP (Turn The Pages) and go SUTG (Straight Up The Guts)!

Ian Cover

Ian Cover, August 2018

INTRODUCTION

A ditty a day

The 'Ditty'. *Dittius, Dittii, Dittum* [Latin]: new words, old tune.

Back in Adelaide in 1977 my lifelong pal Nasty Nigel Lawrence played about with Mondo Rock hits: *If The Chemistry Is Right* became *If The Chemist Shop is Closed*; and *(gonna break into your) Cool World* became *Gonna Break Into Your Tool Shed*. Later Joelene became *Bulleen, Bulleen*; and Nancy & Lee's *(I'm goin' to) Jackson* became *I'm goin' to Chadstone*. We amused each other in this way. Changing existing lyrics for a laugh turned into an accidental 'career' of sorts for me.

In 1983 I began reciting footy poems on *The Coodabeen Champions*—thanks to an introduction from Billy Baxter. In '84, Michael at Melbourne's community radio station, 3RRR, came up with a ditty: *The Answer my Friend, is Like Kicking Into the Wind*. When I tweaked it and sang it on air the other *Coodabeens*—Jeff Richardson, Ian Cover, Simon Whelan and Tony Leonard—told me: "Forget the poetry. That's your role from now on." And I obeyed. I'm now in my 36th year of singing ditties with the *Coodabeens*, most of that time on ABC radio—with a 10-year spell on 3AW in the middle period. Thank you, Michael.

Each week our listeners email around 50 to 80 suggestions. I answer all emails and look for the suggestions that appeal the most. For the past 15 years I generally do about eight ditties each program, four in each hour. Sometimes they're eight fresh ones, or if it's a quiet ideas week, I top up with some of the favourites from the past. Sometimes I cook up the ditty idea by myself and at times I make up the music too. I used to get away with nearly no preparation for the radio show, for the first 20 years or so. Now it takes 8 to 10 hours each week to answer all the messages and cook up new songs.

In the mid-late 90s Stuart Macarthur emerged as the chief listener–contributor of ditties. He was soon joined by the gifted John Ogge and Jane Harris. Somewhere in the mid-late 2000s, Richard Evans came off the rookie list with a bang and emerged as a 200-300 ditty player.

When I spot a listener's suggestions that show ditty-writing talent, I try to nurture and encourage them. I see it as just like young footy players: they

17.5.94 — THAT'S THE THING ABOUT ~~FOOTBALL~~

V1: I get my scarf, got my old coat
I've got a footy game to go to
Footy's on, footy's back again
Here to greet me like an old friend
                and

That's the thing about
"   what I like about
"   the thing about
      "   "   "   football

V2: I'll meet a friend outside the ground
We'll stand together right 'til the end
He'll go for his team, I for mine
We'll disagree on who's gonna win
~~That's what football means to me~~
~~That's how I like my footy to be~~
                and

~~CHORUS~~
Show me the crowd & I'll take my place
I'm hungry, hungry for the ~~taste~~ of it
                and
CHORUS.

M: That's what ~~football~~ means to me
That's how I like my footy to be,
                an'
CHORUS.

V3: I got a long road to walk down
to ~~catch~~ a train to my favourite ground
use my legs, use my voice
make some noise, support the boys
That's what f'ball means ~~to me~~ ......
~~CHORUS~~

Scribble, and dated, for *That's The Thing About Football* (page 60)

may doubt they're going to play at the top level, but bit by bit their skills and self-belief grow. I suspect many a good ditty writer has been lost by sending one or two average ones and not persevering. Some Rising Stars who have emerged as long time contributors are Noel Dennison from Traralgon, Patti from Reservoir, Peter Sim, Doug Long, Peter Treseder and David Blom. We began having catch-ups with this group of nine; that fostered a team feeling and evolved into an email chat group where ditty ideas get workshopped—with good results.

If any email contributor has been overlooked, my sincere apologies. Some of these lyrics go back to 1983 and listener suggestions may well have been lost in the mists of time. A massive thank you to the untold number of listeners who've sent ideas just in the past 15 years alone. That number would be around 18,000 emails, with some prolific contributors like Greg Tuck having sent well over a thousand!

In the early years there were more "characters of the game" such as Dermie, Dipper, Rhys-Jones and Gary senior to write about. One mantra that filtered through from the *Coodabeens* ideology was: *keep it on the field*—focus on the players and the teams. Footy politics and the footy media run a poor second as a ditty topic. In recent decades song themes have become less about individuals and more about hooks that amuse us.

It had never occurred to me or anyone else, to put together a book of these lyrics. I have Geoff Slattery to thank for that—only two and a half weeks ago! I started at Adelaide University aged 17 in 1972, doing an Arts degree with a leaning to English and Australian literature. One dream was to write songs with an Aussie subject matter.

Instead of *Never Going Back to Nashville* or *I Left my Heart in San Francisco*, I imagined *Never Going Back to Dubbo* and *I Left My Heart in Coober Pedy*. A number of those notions did indeed get written; and somewhere along the line the train ran off the tracks and the ideas skewed into ditties about footy.

My only wish is this collection brings you a smile.

Greg Champion

Greg Champion, August 2018

THE 1980s

What began in 1977 in Parkside, an inner suburb of Adelaide as a way to amuse ourselves—changing the lyrics for a laugh, with lifelong pal Nasty Nigel Lawrence—suddenly got called into action in 1984 on community radio 3RRR's *The Coodabeen Champions*.

After an early contributor named Michael suggested *the answer my friend is like kicking into the wind*, I was set on a lifelong course of creating ditties/parodies. In the next seven years we, *The Coodabeens* released about ten cassettes. The order was, I think: '84: *The Better of The Coodabeen Champions*, '85: *In The Outer*, '86: *In The Superbox*, '87: *On The Bench*; 1987-90 then saw the release of *The Double White*, *Back to Back*, *The Cricket Tape I* and *The Cricket Tape II*, and *Phone Calls I* and *Phone Calls II*.

To this day people still talk about those 'golden days' of RRR's Saturday morning programs: we would literally brush shoulders with the *Punter To Punter* team as they left the studio at 10am as we entered. At 11, *Lawyers Guns & Money* started up. We were invited by ABC radio to switch stations in 1987. After much discussion, I believe we declined. In 1988 they asked again, and *The Coodabeens* accepted. The man who invited us, Clarke Hansen, spoke on air with us last year and told us that after our first ABC program, he received **300** complaints!

← In the days of our pub band *The Fabulaires*, circa 1981. Photo by Leanne Temme.

Knee Reconstruction

WORDS: Greg Champion
TO THE TUNE OF: Eve of Destruction

One of the very early ditties, when the ditty concept was still very fresh.

I recall clearly sitting at the lights at the intersection of Elizabeth and Victoria Streets, outside the Vic Market. Eve of Destruction was playing on the radio of my Renault 16. I thought how easily the song's title blended with the common footballer's curse: the knee reconstruction.

The doctor said your knee is gone
there's no point in pretending you can carry on
your ligament is broken in two
there's just one thing I can recommend for you

And he's telling me over and over and over again my friend
I'm going to need a complete knee reconstruction
I'm going to need a complete knee reconstruction

Think of all the knees twisted bent and broken
Think of all the words about knee injuries that are spoken
You may wanna play football till your dying day
But if your knee's had the gong there is no running away

I came out of the plaster three weeks from the date
That medial ruptured and it sealed my fate
The doctor said son, your knee's looking great
Don't worry boy, only twelve more months to wait
You may miss a whole year of football my friend
And when you return your knee just packs up again

And he's telling me over and over and over again my friend
I'm going to need a complete knee reconstruction
I'm going to need a complete knee reconstruction

Mad Micky Malthouse

WORDS: Greg Champion
TO THE TUNE OF: Puff the magic dragon

From about 1984. Mick is most familiar and comfy with his ditty. I've been next to Mick twice at functions and he's very pleasant company. Very different from the fearsome image presented in post-match interviews, *and* when he was playing. Who is the real Mick? Both, possibly.

Mad Micky Malthouse
used to play VFL
but deep down in his brain somewhere
Mick just wasn't well

He'd play a backman's game, old Mick
the ball was his objective
and if someone else should get there first
he'd render them ineffective

He'd shepherd his opponent
and leave 'em more dead than alive
and wonder why on Tuesday night
they rubbed him out for five

He'd play a rugged game old Mick
bumpin' tacklin' crushin'
then something would come over Mick
and he'd give some bloke concussion

Now Mick he played it hard but fair – (but hard)
but Mick was growing older
'til one sad day in eighty-two
he dislocated his shoulder

Sadly Micky Malthouse
gave the game away
but if he makes a comeback
won't you keep out of his way

Oh, mad Micky Malthouse
used to play VFL
but deep down in his brain somewhere
Mick just wasn't well

Amazing Dakes

WORDS: Greg Champion
TO THE TUNE OF: Amazing Grace

In 36 years of radio with the Coodabeen Champions, you meet quite a lot of past champions. Peter Daicos, aka Dakes, is about as natural and pleasant as any human you're ever likely to meet. He doesn't see himself as a star. Footy fans may disagree.

Amazing Dakes, how fleet of foot
how cleverly he plays
if I didn't follow Collingwood
I'd praise him anyway

I used to be a heathen blind
Didn't follow the black and white
Then Daicos came and my heart was claimed
I saw the Magpie light

There is no other team on Earth
To rival Collingwood
And the Pies shall reign over everything
Because they are so good

Amazing Dakes, he floats around
His feet do not toucheth to the ground
I bless the day he came to stay
His Magpie home he found

Amazing Dakes, how quick of hand
And everything he does
Is done with the utmost casualness
Like he's not even trying (!)

I Made A Hundred In The Backyard At Mum's

Greg Champion [BMG Publishing]

The song that started it all, in a way. It arose from a phone chat with my brother about the Aussie Test team's failures in England. I said to him: "The only hundred I ever made was in the backyard at mum's."

I got off the phone and wrote some quick lines. Macca on Australia All Over 'strangled the living suitcase out of it' from 1986. It charted as a single [highest in Queensland] and made me think: gee—maybe I CAN be a songwriter. Still wondering.

As I went out to have a bat just the other day
I had no idea what was coming my way
I played a chanceless innings and I earnt every run
And I made a hundred in the backyard at mum's

Chorus:
Oh, I made a hundred in the backyard at mum's
I clobbered and I crunched every fabulous run
I toiled and I sweated and when the day was done
I'd made a hundred in the backyard at mum's

I started out real shaky like, just poking around
Me sister with her offbreaks, well she had me pinned down
But when me little brother bowled I gave him the clout
And when we stopped for lunch I was twenty-four not out

Then me Uncle Nev came on bowling his quicks
but I was scoring freely with deflections and flicks
as I passed me fifty I paused for ginger beer
and when I hit the roof next door they all began to cheer

I took some on the body, but they didn't hurt a bit
I only hit the ball that was there to be hit
I hooked 'em off me eyebrows and I tried to keep me head
And the ton came up with a straight drive through the window of the shed

Left Hook By Rhys-Jones

WORDS: Greg Champion
TO THE TUNE OF: Peace train

Of all the players we've sung about on the radio, I've often said that David Rhys-Jones has the most right to be aggrieved. But is he? Naaah! He couldn't be less bothered. Smashing chap, socially. Couldn't meet a nicer fella. Mind you, I didn't meet him during the 1987 Grand Final. But David—we salute you. From 1988.

Now he's been cryin' lately
thinkin' about his tribunal fears
and we've seen him sittin' on the bench now
chokin' back a couple of tears

And he's been tryin' harder
to keep his nose clean it seems
but trouble just seems to dog him
what a tough time eighty-eight's been

And Rhys-Jones gets a bit madder
look out for Rhys-Jones
Rhys-Jones is running harder
he's gonna break a few bones

Now Rhys-Jones is tryin' to clean up
He wants to turn a new leaf
but the first sign of any aggro
David quickly comes to grief

Now his form's been down lately
struggled to make the side
but he will turn the corner
he can reverse the tide

And Rhys-Jones does his 'nana
direct hit by Rhys-Jones
quick left and right by Rhys-Jones
out goes someone's lights

Now he's looked so depressed
on occasions when he's been dragged
but Rhys could win the Brownlow
if he wasn't such a dag

And Rhys-Jones goes a bit mental
straight left from Rhys-Jones
two quick jabs by Rhys-Jones
Rhys-Jones is booked again

And Rhys-Jones is in there swingin'
left hook by Rhys-Jones
quick combination by Rhys-Jones
upper cut by Rhys-Jones

Dermott Brereton Is A Hood

Greg Champion [BMG publishing]

We were watching the 1986 Brownlow, and Dermie appeared, and I said to my friend: "See that guy—he is a hood!" This song idea was born then.

I always saw it as a brief, throwaway ditty but it's still the most requested song since it all began. Dermie has been very good-natured about it. He once asked if I could change the lyric "classic Aussie knucklehead"— because, he said, his Mum didn't like it. I said nup. He took it well.

Robbie Flower is a champion
Rioli is a star
But they don't break legs like
big Paul Van Der Haar
Tommy Alvin is a beauty
Mark Arceri is reasonably good
Jimmy Jess is Jimmy Jess
But Dermott Brereton is a hood

Dermott Brereton is a hood
Dermott Brereton is a hood
A bloke that comes from Frankston
Could never be any good
I wouldn't try to tell ya
If I didn't think I should
he's your classic Aussie knucklehead
Dermott Brereton is a hood

Now some folks catch the umpy's eye
Some just do their jobs
Some are trim and fit and some are slobs
Some are quite intelligent
Some misunderstood
Some are well brought up
But Dermott Brereton is a hood

Dermott Brereton is a hood
Dermott Brereton is a hood
A bloke that comes from Frankston
Could never be any good
I wouldn't try to tell ya
If I didn't think I should
he's your classic Aussie knucklehead

Dermott Brereton is a hood

He's your great big hairy punce and
Dermott Brereton is a hood

I'm A Receiver

WORDS: Tony Leonard–Doug Ring–Greg Champion
TO THE TUNE OF: I'm a Believer

From the 1986 cassette, *In The Superbox*. One of the five or six most remembered ditties from the eighties. Tony was not only a key early Coodabeen, he had a knack with ditties also.

I thought football was more or less an easy thing
Tough for someone else, but not for me
What's the use in tryin'
All you get is pain
Not for those who have a football brain

I create the space
I'm a receiver
it's just a case
of using your mind
I run wide – ooo
I'm a receiver
I'm the receiver of the side

I thought football was more or less just havin' a kick
And diving into packs was not for me
Can't afford to get injured
You know I dislike pain
Never won a vote in a vital game

I create the space
I'm a receiver
it's just a case
of using your mind
I run wide – ooo
I'm a receiver
I'm the receiver of the side

My Homeground

WORDS: Greg Champion
TO THE TUNE OF: My Hometown

From 1989. Maybe the first heavily sentimental piece from *The Coodabeens*.
It still gets me, today. It shows me not all ditties are flippant—just most.

In '85, the Dogs had come alive
At finals time
We were steering straight, with Tony Capes
Was a stirring time, at my home ground

In '87 the party's gone
The club had come undone
Things went strange, winds of change
Troubled times had come

To my home ground, my home ground
my home ground

In '88 they closed the gates
After the final round
Empty stands, devoid of fans
No more siren sound

At my home ground, in Footscray town
they shut it down, my home ground

Now the clubrooms have cracked windows
And boarded doors
Seems like nobody wants to
Go down there no more
But me I still remember
the way that day
The President announced the Doggies
would no longer play

At my home ground, my home ground
my home ground

Now my kids kick a ball
Round the empty ground
And sometimes I go
Down and take a good look around

At my home ground, my home ground

On Corio Bay

WORDS: Greg Champion
TO THE TUNE OF: Morningtown Ride

From around 1990, this was the first of many Cats-themed songs.
It still gets a smile when sung, especially around Sleepy Hollow.

Driving down the freeway
past the Ford Factory
going to Moor-a-bool Street
to watch the great Gary

Off to see the Hooped Affair
at Kardinia Park
where everybody goes to bed
as soon as it gets dark

Will they cop a hiding
will they win the day
for all the fans at Geelong Town
on Corio Bay

There's a Gary in the engine room
a Gary who kicks goals
Barnesy rucks his heart out
and Billy runs hot and cold

Somewhere there's an Ocean Grove
Somewhere there's Norlane
Somewhere there's a Geelong flag
many miles away

Will they cop a hiding
will they win the day
for all the fans at Geelong Town
on Corio Bay

Playin' For The Saints

WORDS: Matthew Hardy–Greg Champion
TO THE TUNE OF: Puttin' On the Ritz

From the mid-eighties era when a number of Carlton cast-offs would end their careers with a year or two at the Saints.

If you're a Blue
and you don't know where to go to
why don't you come down with your mates
Playin' for the Saints

If you're short of a yard
and you don't want to have to try so hard
you'll have lots of mates
Playin' for the Saints

Dressed up like a million dollar rover
even if your playing days are over

Different types who wear what they
like to training some who don't
turn up when it's raining
Playin' for the Saints

They've got vacancies in key positions
'specially if you like the wet conditions

If training seems like hard work
and getting dropped again is
one of your pet hates
Come and join the Saints

Johnny Gastev

WORDS: Greg Champion
TO THE TUNE OF: Yellow River

In the early days—probably 1988 here—I had a habit of paying tribute to the lesser lights, the foot soldiers.

Who's the toast of old Brisbane town
Who could play with his shorts pulled down
Who keeps pulling the screamers down
Is it Martin Leslie?

Who's the King of the Gold Coast scene
Face is on every magazine
Glamour boy of the suntan team
Is it Matty Rendell?

No it's Johnny Gastev, Johnny Gastev
He's dead-eye dick, he's terrific
Johnny Gastev, Johnny Gastev
His fuzzy hair bobs up everywhere

Who's the Bear who's a coach's dream
Who's the one man fighting machine
Always where the ball's just been
Is it Stephen Reynoldson?

And when the Bears find themselves behind
Ten goals down and it's quarter time
Who comes on like a raging lion
Is it Mark Zanotti?

No it's Johnny Gastev, Johnny Gastev
He's a care Bear for Normie Dare
Johnny Gastev, Johnny Gastev
Another kick to Mister Magic

All Along The Boundary Line

WORDS: Greg Champion
TO THE TUNE OF: All along the watchtower

From the late eighties.

I am a member of the umpire clan
a disdained man in white
sometimes the pressure of the job
means I don't sleep at night
I suffer white line fever
I run a narrow line
and if the ball goes out of play
I get it every time

And I'll be all along the boundary line
that's where my work will be
'cos throwin' in balls when they're out of bounds
that's what's important to me
I hold the ball up vertical
take my position and then
when I'm ready to do my thing –
then I just throw it in!

I've come down from the country
I have but one desire
to make it big in The Big Smoke
as a serious boundary umpire
And when the weekend rolls around
I become all uptight
I'll take the field at Princes Park
but I'll be outa sight

And I'll be all along the boundary line
that's where my work will be
'cos throwin' in balls when they're out of bounds
that's what's important to me
Goalpost to goalpost
my world begins and ends
the only thing I have to do is
throw the football in!

I'm DiPierdomenico

WORDS: Greg Champion
TO THE TUNE OF: I'm Henry the Eighth

This tune became quite popular in 1986 and then…Dipper won the Brownlow. That just helped kick it along. We put out a cassette single! Every time we *Coodabeens* see Dipper he asserts: "I made you blokes"! We respond that it is we who made him. This has been going on for thirty years…

I'm DiPierdomenico DiPierdomenico-o ho ho
I go in hard and I leave them sore
Been reported seven times before
and every one was an accident [accident!]
just a case of bad luck
and I'm always ready to have a go, I'm DiPierdomenico

I'm DiPierdomenico, spreading trouble wherever I go
I'm a part of the Hawthorn style
been a Hawk for a long, long while
I've never played for Essendon [Essendon!]
never was a Swan or a Cat
I am Robert DiPierdomenico, I'm Dippy – take that !

I'm DiPierdomenico, how you spell that I don't know
I like boring into packs
and breaking up opposition attacks
I'm never violent deliberately [deliberately!]
I just get carried away
I am Robert DiPierdomenico, and that's how I'll stay

I'm DiPierdomenico, how I got to be, I don't know
they just stuck me on a wing
and asked me to do my Domenico thing
and anyone that comes near me [comes near me!]
they wipe out with a splat
and they call me DiPierdomenico, I'm Dippy – and that's that

I'm DiPierdomenico, all the way from head to toe
You've probably heard my name
I've been rubbed out for a dozen games
and everyone was a man I hit [a man I hit!]
I never hit a Lily or a Pam
I'm Sir Robert DiPierdomenico – that's who I am!

Dougie Hawkins

WORDS: Greg Champion–Steve Burton–John Kelly
TO THE TUNE OF: Swanee

In the mid-eighties, paying tribute to the game's most popular players was the thing to do.

Dougie, how we love ya, how we love ya, our Dougie Hawkins
He puts the other wingmen to shame plays his own game
Got that mad stare not quite all there
When he hits his stride they step aside for our Dougie Hawkins
He is a legend, amongst Doggie fans, the hero of the Footscray stands

Dougie, how we love ya, how we love ya our Dougie Hawkins
He gets the ball and runs 'round in rings, love to watch him
when he's hot no-one can touch him
How good, just how good, how very good is our Dougie Hawkins
He doesn't mind those whacks 'round the ears
Here's to you Dougie and three cheers

Dougie, scores from way out, never in doubt, our Dougie Hawkins
He is the idol of Barkly Street, kicks with both feet
watch that left hook he's from Braybrook
Dougie, pulls them in under his chin does our dear old Dougie
We love those marks with only one hand, yes Dougie Hawkins is our man

Dougie, loves to tackle, sell the dummy, our Dougie Hawkins
His blood it flows with red white & blue, likes a beer too
or three or four or even more and
Dougie, 'round the packs and in the action, go for it Dougie
When Footscray needs that someone to lead
Dougie's there to do the deed

Dougie, what a player, lives in Footscray, our dear old Dougie
with number seven stuck on his back, breaks up the pack
and turns defence into attack and
Dougie, should be captain of the Doggies, our Dougie Hawkins
When things look grim he comes to the fore
and wins it for the Dogs once more

Robbie Flower Can

WORDS: Greg Champion
TO THE TUNE OF: The Candyman

The reverence in which Robbie Flower was held by the football-loving public was, perhaps, unique.

Who can make the ball talk
Handle it with love
Here's a little clue he plays on the wing
Robbie Flower can
Robbie Flower can
'cos he seems to have the ball on the end of a string

Who can weave his magic
Dazzle you with style
Wears the red and blue and always has done too
Robbie Flower can
Robbie Flower can
'cos the things that he can do, he can make you smile

There is no opponent he can't handle
No-one to him can hold a candle
Thrills the crowd with each appearance
Never ever sought a clearance

Who can turn a game 'round
Off his own boot
Talented, terrific and clever and cute
Robbie Flower can
Robbie Flower can
'cos he's football's Mr Magic there is no dispute

There is no-one quite like Robbie Flower

Rossie Thornton Has A Football Brain

WORDS: Greg Champion

Fitzroy was everyone's second team in the mid-eighties. Rossie Thornton, yet another of Fitzroy's Western Districts products, was one of many likeable players for the Lions. I met him recently and he's just as likeable today!

There is a team that in modern times
has had an arduous uphill climb
with no social club and no homeground
it's a mystery how they're still around

They've had their heroes who've come and gone
and names like Quinlan will linger on
Garry Wilson was a handy sort
and Leon Harris gives his all to the sport

But there's one player at the Lions club
he's not big and strong, I'll give ya the rub
but he's got something that's hard to explain
Rossie Thornton has a football brain

Now Leigh Carlson played with courage and nerve
and finished his days off in the reserves
but one thing the fans are still dying to know is
why'd they ever let Bradley Gotch go

They've shifted home grounds, they've changed their coach
Leon Wiegard's tried to keep them afloat
at least their back pocket gives 'em some bite
he shines bright like a light in the night

He may not have played three hundred games
doesn't have the hairstyle of a Lee Murnane
but never sell this man down the drain
because Rossie Thornton has a football brain

He does the obvious he does it well
you show him the dummy he'll show you the sell
don't do dramatic things that's not his game
but – Rossie Thornton has a football brain

The Day The Goal Ump Went The Screamer

Greg Champion [BMG Publishing]

Somewhere in the early nineties, I was listening to a game on radio and the commentator said: "... and the ball sails into the goalsquare and—WOOOOHHH!!!"
 And as a listener, you think—what!? Has the goal umpy come out and taken a screamer??

Now there was never a sight so surprising
So absurd yet so debonair
As the day the goal ump went the screamer
And pulled down the mark of the year

Do you recall the way it all happened
How the build-up began at half-back
And as the ball sailed into the goal square
Guess who should fly over the pack

Well he seemed to just hang there for ages
Like a dazzling Ablett in white
And with his long umpy coat, and his hat still on
He pulled in the pill with one bite

And there was never a sight so surprising
So absurd and outrageous as well
As the day the goal ump went the screamer
And flew like a startled gazelle

Now the crowd broke into an uproar
And others just stood there in shock
But the field umpy just blew his whistle
So the goal ump went back for his shot

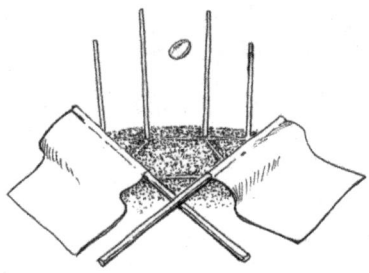

Now the fans all began to enjoy it
So they cheered this astonishing bloke
And as the ball sailed through and out of the ground
On their hotdogs they did choke

So he went for a lap of the oval
To enraptured applause from the fans
And as he waved to the crowd, with his smile big and proud
They were falling about in the stands

So he gave a boundary line interview
Then promptly went back to his end
And every goal that sailed through and the ump stuck up two
They cheered him all over again

Now there was never a sight so surprising
So absurd yet so debonair
As the day the goal ump went the screamer
And pulled down the mark of the year

The Springtime It Brings On The Finals

WORDS: Greg Champion

I met Cove and Billy in 1980 when Cove was booking the bands at The Ozone pub, Queenscliff. The pair were inseparable. And for our band the Fabulaires, boy, was The Ozone ever an H.H.G: happy hunting ground. Did that pub go off!

In 1983 Billy had a midweek show on 3RRR. He let me come on air and read some footy poems I'd been writing. He said: "I'm going to introduce you to the *Coodabeen Champions*." *The Coodabeens* graciously allowed a stranger to come on air on a Saturday morning and recite footy poems.

They allowed that to continue for roughly a year—until I sang my first on-air parody. I can hear Cove and Tony now, telling me: "That's it for the poems. You're doing songs from now on." A few of the poems survive, and this is one Richo still likes to play annually come finals time.

The springtime it brings on the finals
the blossom is on the trees
the players are in the changerooms
getting injections in their cute little knees

Attendants are all at the turnstiles
letting people in one by one
goal umpies between the goalposts
and the whole joint's full of fun

Flags are flyin' from the stands
there are streamers hats and balloons
and mums and kids and business types
and mobs of drunken hoons

People walk with quicker step
there's magic in the air
see you out at Waverley
you're a mug if you don't get there

The birds fly 'round the MCG
they don't have to be told
they're all decked out in Lions colours
and some in brown and gold

The bees are buzzing 'round the flowers
they've been waiting 'round for a week
they seem to say "c'mon the Bombers"
but we know bees don't really speak

I love those footy finals
what an avant garde idea
whoever invented footy finals
get that star a beer

The Mad Stare Of The Half-Back Flanker

WORDS: Greg Champion [1983]

A chief source of inspiration for footy poems in 1983 was a chance remark from a commentator. I was watching mid-week night footy from Waverley when I wrote down Louie Richards' comment about a visiting WA player: "He's a tear-through type this bloke—he's got that mad stare about him".

I was watching the Escort Cup
On a frozen Tuesday night
When something Louie said
Had a ring that rang just right

Some team was over from WA
They were going pretty strong
And one of their defenders
Just couldn't put a foot wrong

And Lou was heard to say
In a way that you could not doubt him
He's a tear-through type this bloke
He's got that mad stare about him

Cruising through the night
Llike a giant oil tanker
Only a few can wear
The mad stare of the half-back flanker

Dippy had it and he knew it
So did Billy Picken
Particularly when he was kickin'
To the legendary Steven Icken

Like Crazy Horse Cowton
They're the ones who show the signs
That deranged kind of attitude
That quality hard to find

Sailing ever onwards
like a giant oil tanker
Only a few can wear
the mad stare of the half-back flanker

I Love A Sunburnt Country Football Oval

WORDS: Greg Champion

One of the first poems—from 1983-84. It's on our second cassette *Another Side of the Coodabeen Champions*.

I love a sunburnt country football oval
'cos that's the place where footy's played out there
and if you like our noble game of footy
to honour where it's played, is only fair

I love a rambling rural football oval
especially when the grass is oh so green
and lofty goalposts stretch towards the heavens
and a picket fence, setting off the scene

Each week the cars will park around the flanks
while farmer battles farmer in the ring
and people blow their horns for every goal
and really get involved in what they're doing

Red Hot Go

Greg Champion [BMG publishing]

Around the late eighties *The Coodabeens* became infatuated with some of the key clichés of football, such as the red hot go [RHG]. We flogged them in the on-air banter and I recall clearly, a punter at a live gig said to me: you should put all those acronyms in a song. That might never have occurred to me. What a top thought; so I did. I also recall the first night we sang it, live to a radio audience in Newcastle. It got instant beaut reaction, especially from the *Coodas*. Gordon Bennett at Chanel Seven employed it as a theme for a while on a Sunday morning footy talk show.

We were playin' footy
For the *Coodabeens*
In our annual match
Against South Merbein
We were gettin' flogged
Things were pretty crook
When someone yelled out
Take a good hard look

Then we **TTC** – turned the corner
Had an **RHG** – red hot go
Yeah, we **OTFG** – opened the floodgates
We got **BIT** – back in town
We **LOG** – lifted our game
And took a good hard look at ourselves

Well the coach came out – **O.U.T.**
He said you're **JG** – just going
He made a **BS** – big statement
Said it's a **WNBG** – whole new ball game
He said you're **LDTB** – looking down the barrel
And take a **GHLAY**

Then we **TTC** – turned the corner
Had an **RHG** – red hot go
Yeah, we **TCAP** – threw the cat amongst the pigeons
We got **BIT** – back in town
We **STD** – spat the dummy
And took a good hard look at ourselves

My game had been bad – **B.A.D.**
In fact I'd had an **AS** – absolute shocker
The coach pulled me out – **O.U.T.**
Said I had an **AP** – attitude problem
He said you've **DYB** – dropped your bundle
And take a **GHLAY**

Then we **TTC** – turned the corner
Had an **RHG** – red hot go
VMSB – very much so Bobby
We got **BIT** – back in town
We **STD** – spat the dummy
And took a good hard look at ourselves

Refrain:
We were **H&H** – home & hosed
It was an **HHG** – happy hunting ground
We got **BTB** – back to basics
TLTB – thank you linesmen thank you ballpersons
We were **CP**s – consummate professionals
We **TNFS** – thrust our names in front of the selectors
We **GEI** – gave every indication
We got **BTB** – back to basics
And took a good hard look at ourselves

THE 1990s

After one year at ABC radio Dear Old Auntie invited *The Coodabeen Champions* to do a three-hour Sunday evening program, nationally. What a pleasure and privilege. We enjoyed 19 years presenting our national evening show on the ABC. There was a break from 1996-2002 when *The Coodabeens* switched to 3AW. The ditties continued regardless, or "irregardless" as the *Coodabeens* like to say. In 1994 I/we released the first CD of footy songs, *That's What I Like About Football Vol I*. Volume II followed in 1995. For the 20 or so years of the show I only did one song on air per week—occasionally two. That changed in 2003 when *The Coodabeens* moved back to ABC radio. It was 1999 when I made a third footy CD, this time with a few more serious original songs on it. It also included phone calls from Tony's talkback.

← Grand Final Day 1995. On the 'G. The blurred head behind me is that of the hugely loved, immortal, Wayne Duncan, on bass. On stage with me that day were The Coodabeens, Ian Cover, Tony Leonard, Simon Whelan, Jeff Richardson. In the band were Gary Carruthers, Wayne Duncan, Geoff Hassall and Sam See.

The Day That Richmond Wins The Flag

WORDS: Greg Champion
TO THE TUNE OF: Green, green grass of home

Late in 2017 I saw a tweet quoting some old lyrics of mine, of which I had no memory. It was from Mary Bolling, so I asked her could she estimate the year, and she said about 1995. I was very pleased to find the words in the old files.

Swan Street still looks the same
as you gaze down from the train
And there stands Dimmeys and the grunge pub on the corner
and they haven't triumphed in September
for so long, most cannot remember
It's decades since, the Tigers won a flag

They'll be partyin' and smilin'
from the Central Club down to Herring Island
on the day that Richmond wins the flag

Now Church Street will explode
and they'll have to close Bridge Road
In Victoria Street the Vietnamese will party
and the Skipping Girl will prance all night
The Punt Road ground will be a hallowed sight
on the day that Richmond wins the flag

They'll be rollin' and a-rockin'
from the high-rise flats to the Nylex Clock
They'll paint the town when Richmond wins the flag

They'll be partyin' and smilin'
from the Central Club down to Herring Island
on the day that Richmond wins the flag

Deep In Our Hearts Everyone Barracks For Fitzroy

Greg Champion [BMG Publishing]

I would venture this idea came up while watching footy around 1990, and it may have been a narrow loss for Fitzroy—or just something endearing about the Lions' style and their history—but it was very hard not to like Fitzroy. Everybody's second team.

Oh, deep in our hearts everyone barracks for Fitzroy
Whether we say we barrack for someone else or not
Yeah, deep in our hearts everyone barracks for Fitzroy
Because Fitzroy is the most loveable team we've got

Now if Fitzroy was the only team within the Football League
I don't think anybody would be seriously aggrieved [except for Collingwood]
They'd still play their games out with character and flair
Even if the opposition simply was not there

Now Fitzroy as a team are a fairly good bunch
Except for Darren Wheildon you could take 'em home to lunch
They're well presented well-behaved, they cause no offence
With the possible exception of James Manson

Now Fitzroy is the team in the red, gold and blue
There's a little bit of me in them and I know there's some of you
There's a little bit of everybody else you know too
And if you want to lose to one team then it's Fitzroy

Yes, deep in our hearts everyone barracks for Fitzroy
Whether we say we barrack for someone else or not
Yeah, deep in our hearts everyone barracks for Fitzroy
Because Fitzroy is the most loveable team we've got

Twisted Club Songs

WORDS: Greg Champion

It seemed a simple fun idea to mess with the club songs and their lyrics. Kevin Sheedy once stopped me in Yarra Park and said: "Those Essendon songs with the different tunes—can I get a copy of those?" Very happy to oblige.

TO THE TUNE OF: COLLINGWOOD CLUB SONG

Good old Essendon forever
we are rich and we are great
we're establishment in Melbourne
we own real estate
With our Catholic tradition
we will win with ease
oh, the premiership's a prayer away
for the Essendon diocese!

TO THE TUNE OF: CARLTON CLUB SONG

We are from Essendon
we are from smack bang Essendon
We're from up Mt Alexander way
just proceed along past Moonee Ponds
up through the junction
then you'll arrive at our lavish function
We're Western suburbs but we're genteel
Oh, we're the famous Essendon

TO THE TUNE OF: GEELONG CLUB SONG

We are the Pies
the greatest team of all
all other teams do not count at all
We play the game just as we choose
'cos we are better than youse
No-one is half as good as Collingwood
and you know what youse can do

The Day Big Al Jumped Off The Sydney Harbour Bridge

WORDS: Greg Champion-Greg Tangey
TO THE TUNE OF: Ode to Billy Joe

In 1995 the Pies had to beat Sydney, away, in the last round to make the finals. They lost. Big Al carried on.

It was the third of September, a sleepy sort of Father's Day
Collingwood was well in front and looked liked kicking away
And after lunch we turned it off to take the dog out for a stroll
And Mama hollered at the back door Plugger's kicked a few, they're on a roll
Then she yelled the Pies are gone, and she went and grabbed a beer from the fridge
The day Big Al McAlister jumped off the Sydney Harbour Bridge

Papa said to mama as he passed around the Kraft Cheddar cheese
Well, Big Al never had a lick of sense, pass the bottle opener please
There's gonna be some blood lettin' down at Victoria Park now
And mama said that she was sad about Big Al anyhow
Seems like nothing ever works out right down at Collingwood
And now Big Al McAllister's gone and said goodbye for good

Mama says to me, I feel sorry 'bout them black and whites
They always seem to think that the umpies never treat 'em right
I saw that nice young Tony Shaw on telly just the other day
Said he'd be pleased to coach Collingwood next year, and by the way
He said to make the finals they would have to lose some excess bagg-age
And he and Big Al were throwing something off the Studley Park swing bridge

A week has come and gone since we heard the news about Big Al
The best eight teams in the comp, are in the finals now
Bombers have made it, Carlton's trying for another one
And mama's acting strange, and not barracking for anyone
Me I spend a lot of time picking daisies 'round Studley Park
And drop them into the Yarra water near the Burnley overpass

Good Old Collingwood II

WORDS: Greg Champion

Good old Collingwood however
They don't always win the game
Side by side they stuck together
But they still went down in flames
See the barrackers a-shouting
That the umpires are to blame
Oh the Premiership's a pipedream
As the Pies go down again

A Lotta People Care About Richmond

Greg Champion [BMG Publishing]

These thoughts bob up watching the footy: the Tigers are going through a lean trot—for about thirty-five years. Around 1999 a Tigers game was on—and they goaled. The camera showed a horde of joyful Tiges fans. And you realise—despite years of low ladder finishes, there are a whole lot of people who love Richmond.

At the Punt Rd end of the Southern Stand
they raise their arms and cheer
the Tiger faithful will persist,
until it is their year
They don't mind how long they wait
they'll be ready to celebrate
Love 'em or not it's plain there's a lot
of people who care about Richmond

To the London Tavern from Bridge Rd
it's a stroll down Lennox Street
When you wander round this Richmond Town
who knows what you might meet
They come from every side of the track
but they're unified in the gold and black
Love 'em or not it's plain there's a lot
of people who care about Richmond

Well, I don't know when their time will come
but it surely won't be long
'til we hear that Tiger army sing that
famous gold & black song
And their loyalty will be repaid
one fine September Saturday
Love 'em or not it's plain there's a lot
of people who care about Richmond

And you can see 'em on your TV
and they look like you and me
Patiently awaiting, their date with history
Love 'em or not it's plain there's a lot of
of people who care about Richmond

Don't Let The Big V Down

Greg Champion [BMG Publishing]

The Coodabeens' interactions with the great EJ (Teddy) Whitten were always a delight. I once saw him speak at the Dandenong Football Club. More laughs than any comedian. Teddy needed a recording of the Big V song—so he joined us in the recording studio. He was a tornado of energy. He sang with such gusto. The tale is told how he made this comment, the song title, to a first-time player for Victoria, in the changerooms. Teddy's final lap of the 'G in 1995, accompanied by Ted junior, may be the most emotional moment that footy will ever provide.

A young man in the changeroom
Reflecting on his fate
Trying to block the nerves
In his first game for the state
When boldly steps up to him
A Bulldog kinda man
Fixed his eyes upon him
And as he pressed his hand, he said

Don't, don't let the Big V down
Not when EJ's around

The man who shook his hand
Was one of history's best
Who'd built his reputation
As a leader from the West
And leadership he'd given
From then until this day
When he chested up to the new kid
especially to say

Don't, don't let the Big V down
Not when EJ's around

Don't let the Big V down
Don't let the Big V down
It echoed in his head
As he stepped onto the ground
His football said it then
His words are with us now
Don't, Don't let the Big V down
Don't, Don't let the Big V down

VFL Park In The Dark

Greg Champion [BMG Publishing]

A common question is: what tune is it to? None—this one's an original song, and that's a big reason that I'm fond of it.

It was around 1988, and I was watching mid-week footy from Waverley. I'd been listening to Van Morrison's mighty album, *Inarticulate Speech of the Heart*. If you explore that album, you can feel this song seeping through!

Many times people ask, what's your favourite footy song, over the whole journey? I say this one. And plenty of times people volunteer that it's their number one also.

I went to VFL park
I went to VFL park in the dark
let me tell ya –

I saw Bolzon make a mistake on the wing
I bought a hotdog at half-time
I saw the Lions run away in the last term
and John Ironmonger did a one-handed pick-up on the run, and that's fair dinkum

Down at VFL park
It was at VFL park in the dark. And what's more

Gary Pert made a magic save in front of goal
I saw O'Dwyer take a strong mark on a lead
The cheer squad got involved, as the Demons kicked that goal
Just as the siren sounded for half-time

It was at VFL, it was at VFL park in the dark

Now Micky Conlan did several handballs, which was an unusual thing
Keane looked good in patches
Roos is like a Mexican dancer
The Demons, they had no answer – where ?

Down at VFL park
Well, it was at VFL park in the dark
Nowhere else but, VFL park
That's where it was…..VFL park….
Veeeeeeeeeeeee…VFL, VFL, VFL….
It was at VFL park….

Tony Modra's Gone Surfing

WORDS: Greg Champion
TO THE TUNE OF: Surfin' USA

Gee, you wouldn't mind a Tony Modra up front now. It was said that the Dockers picked up 600 South Aussie members when Tony transferred to Freo. In full flight, a genius. Maybe the smartest soccerer to play the game.

Well the Crows said you're out 'cos you didn't turn up to training
And he said "but I had a sore neck, and besides it was raining"
And they said "well you're out for a week, so it's no use complaining"
And he said "fine, fine, fine, 'cos I'm going surfing anyway"

Tony Modra's gone surfing
Victor Harbour way
Tony Modra's gone surfing
South Coast, SA

Well he headed for Victor Harbour and there he did linger
While he checked out the swell from Port Elliot to Waitpinga
Then he surfed every break from Moama to Aldinga
While the Crows played the Swans, Swans, Swans, and the Swans beat 'em anyway

Then he said "well, you're off to Geelong won't ya reinstate me now"
Thinkin' if I go bad I can pop down to Anglesea now
And with the board and the wetsuit I could grab a few waves at Torquay now
And the Crows got done, done, done so he should've surfed anyway

Tony Modra's gone surfing
Victor Harbour way
Tony Modra's gone surfing
He'll be back one day

Gary Ablett Will Reappear In Round Six

WORDS: Greg Champion [BMG publishing]

In 1991 Gary senior retired suddenly, pre-season, shocking the footy world. He was 29. He was convinced to return in round 12. He then played on and starred until injury in the pre-season of 1997 ended a stellar career.

Gary Ablett will reappear in round six
Gary Ablett will reappear in round six
He'll run out with the Cats
Pull a rabbit from his hat
Show off all his old party tricks
Gary Ablett will reappear in round six

Gary Ablett will be called to the Vatican in round nine
Gary Ablett will be called to the Vatican in round nine
He'll be summoned by the pope
On the day he kicks
Thirteen goals before quarter time
Gary Ablett will be called to the Vatican in round nine

Gary Ablett will walk on water in round ten
Gary Ablett will walk on water in round ten
He'll make the ball sit up and talk
And to prove it's no fluke
He'll make it sit back up and talk again
Gary Ablett will walk on water in round ten

Gary Ablett will disappear in round fifteen
Gary Ablett will disappear in round fifteen
He'll go up for the fly
And in the flicker of an eye
There'll just be a puff of smoke where he was last seen
Gary Ablett will disappear in round fifteen

Playing Accountable Football

WORDS: Greg Champion
TO THE TUNE OF: Killing me softly with his song

Way back around 1985 someone sent a ditty, *Killing Us Softly With Handball*. We never did trace that contributor, despite on-air appeals over the years. The lyrics had a certain stream of consciousness to them. In 1997 I recast it, below. These words just make it clear that I was taking a shot at the latest footy jargon as long as twenty-one years ago. Nothing's changed there—it's only become a more frequent theme.

I journeyed to the football
To have a red hot yell
But who was playing where
Was oh so hard to tell
The ploys the coach was using
To me were most confusing

On-ballers flooding the backline
Hard-at-the-contest set plays
Playing accountable football
Running off taggers
And generally using some weird plans
I couldn't understand

I reached out for the *Record*
To work the match-ups out
But every hard ball soft get
left me more in doubt
I just got more befuddled
with every set play huddle

Setting their zones for the kick-off
trying to run through the lines
creating defensive turnovers
getting to more loose ball options
More often, and above all
just being accountable

woh oh, oh...
Playing accountable football
getting to more loose ball options
more often, and above all
just being accountable

Every Day Is A Football Day

Greg Champion [BMG publishing]

Moving to Melbourne from Adelaide in 1979, one key thing I picked up was that *everybody* in Melbourne follows footy. In Adelaide support for the game was kept to certain elements. That may have changed somewhat now, due to the two AFL sides, but you soon learn that footy permeates all strata of society in Victoria. A beautiful thing. Four years after *That's The Thing About Football*, I went back to Mike Brady and we recorded this.

I try to think of something else
but the mind comes back to one thing
who are the ins and outs this week
and where is every team playing
You see it in the faces of
the people at the station
in this town that's just their way
every day is a football day

So bounce the ball and let us play
and we'll dream about September
The woes of the world can fade away
every day is a football day

Not everybody loves the game
and not everybody has to
but if you have it in the blood
then love it's what you must do
So come on let's enjoy the day
down to the ground we'll wander
and life shall be a memory
of an endless game at the MCG

So bounce the ball and let us play
and we'll dream about September
the woes of the world can fade away
every day is a football day

All along Port Phillip Bay
where seagulls wheel among the spray
the weekend's come and all's okay
every day is a football day

Well I Dreamed I Saw

WORDS: Greg Champion–Brian Beesley
TO THE TUNE OF: After the goldrush

From 1999. This shows how long we've been 'bleating' about certain features of the broadcast. Sensory overload was in its infancy—it's reached epidemic status now. At least they hadn't started—I think—switching camera angles then.

Well I dreamed I saw the footy on TV
but it did not look the same
I was sure there was a match on but
I couldn't quite see the game
There was a golden-coloured muffler that
kept rolling across the screen
and out of it sprang these two exhaust pipes
Have you had this dream?

Well I dreamed I saw this whizz-bang techno scoreboard
but I couldn't work out what for
There was scaffolding and computer game graphics
but I could not read the score
All in a dream, all in a dream
A banner flashed across the screen
it was a group of players' names called 'match-ups'
What did all that mean?

I was lying back in my armchair
with the big game on TV
but the scorebox in the corner was
a space age mystery
There was this strange-shaped barrel in gold and black
hanging from the sky
Welcome to the football coverage in nineteen ninety-nine

Spiro Malakellis

WORDS: Greg Champion
TO THE TUNE OF: Living next Door to Alice

From 1992. Ah, they were simpler times: the Malakellis brothers,
Spiro and Tony played together at Geelong in the nineties.

Spiro was raised in a fishing town
By the Adriatic Sea near a soccer ground
Above the Parthenon, just outside Athens
He played with a ball on the streets with the kids
And it soon became clear from the tricks he did
He was going to be … above average

Oh, I don't know how they found him, but I'm just so glad they did
Recruited from the Amos, as a seven-year-old kid
Oh, there's never been a hero, big as Spiro Malakellis
Twenty-four years old and destined for fame
Five foot seven tall and getting shorter every game
No, there's never been a hero, big as Spiro Malakellis

Then one fateful day his Papa came home
He said, "pack up your things, on a journey we're goin'
To the big football ground, Down Under"
To the second biggest Greek community in the world
Where there's plenty of Ouzo and lotsa Greek girls
I'm gonna get a fish and chippery—in Anakie

Oh, I don't know how they found him, but I'm just so glad they did
Recruited from the Amos, as a seven-year-old kid
Oh, there's never been a hero, big as Spiro Malakellis
Twenty-four years old and destined for fame
Five foot seven tall and getting shorter every game
No, there's never been a hero, big as Spiro Malakellis

That's The Thing About Football

Greg Champion [BMG Publishing]–Mike Brady–Paul Kelly

I met Mike Brady at an advertising function around 1993. He suggested we should do a footy song. Six months later I had an idea and I took it to Mike. He said later he didn't like it that much at the time but he kindly worked it up with me. I paid an A-team to record it at Sing Sing. Mike produced, and he came up with the ripper woh woh bit.

I sent it to (the hugely-loved) Gordon Bennett at Ch.7 Sport, and he told me on the phone "I think you're trying to tell too much of a story". (I think he was mentally comparing it to *Up There Cazaly*, which Gordon had made into a hit 15 years earlier). I asked him if he'd listened to it all and he was *honest and gracious* enough to concede that he hadn't. This is what makes Gordon such a legend.

I said that the song builds up towards the end so he said he'd re-listen, and he called back half an hour later saying, "I like it now". The next day Gary Fenton called and made me an offer I couldn't understand (little joke).

The night before we were due to record, I was sweating over the lyrics. I tried to get hold of Paul Kelly to ask for his help. He was away in Adelaide, but I managed to get a fax number and I faxed my lyrics requesting his input. We hadn't spoken. *The next morning at 8AM there on the fax were three four-line verses of lyrics from Paul!!* I only ended up using one line—but it was a goodie—and it was so kind of him to help out so quickly.

I've got my scarf got my old coat
I've got a footy game to go to
Footy's on footy's here again
Back to greet me like an old friend, and

That's the thing about
That's what I like about
That's the thing about, the thing about football, woh-oh

I'll meet a friend outside the ground
We'll argue over who's gonna win
He'll go for his team I for mine
We'll watch 'em slug it out right to the end, and
Show me the crowd and I'll take my place
I'm hungry, I'm hungry for the taste of it, and

That's the thing about
That's what I like about
That's the thing about, the thing about football, woh-oh

That's what football means to me
That's how I like my footy to be, and

I've got a long road to walk down
To catch a tram to my favourite ground
Use my legs, use my voice
Make some noise, support the boys, and
That's what football means to me
That's how I like my footy to be, and

That's the thing about
That's what I like about
That's the thing about, the thing about football, woh-oh

Came From Adelaide

WORDS: Greg Champion
TO THE TUNE OF: I've been everywhere

May I say first, that the tune is written by the wonderful, immortal Geoff Mack. What a charming gentleman he was, and he only left us recently, in July 2017, aged 94. He was extremely gracious about allowing his classic song to be parodied—many times. All who knew him, loved him.

Born in the Melbourne suburb of Surrey Hills, he was schooled at nearby Camberwell Grammar. He made his name as an entertainer abroad, during the Second World War, and he wrote *I've been everywhere* in 1962.

The parody come from the early nineties. This was before internet, so how did I track all those names? I have a hunch footy swap cards may have been used. I did have many of those names on real swap cards as a kid in Adelaide, and saw many of them play.

I was watching my TV with a mate just the other day
He turned to me and said, man those Croweaters just can't play
I turned around and said, mate that just isn't true
South Australians are great, as I'm about to tell you, 'cos

Came from Adelaide man, came from Adelaide man
South Australian made man, drank Woodies lemonade man
Shoulda been there when they played man
Came from Adelaide man – they had

Motley Bradley Peter Jonas what a bonus
John Platten Steven Stretch Craig McKellar what a fella
John Cahill Matt Rendell Milan Faletic so athletic
Mark Williams Russell Ebert Kernahan what a man
Rick Davies Robert Klomp Graham Cornes blow your horns
Phil Maylin Greg Phillips Chris Kellett can't you tell it

ya got -
Philipou Fred Bills Fred Phillis Wayne Phillis
Ken Farmer Lindsay Backman Doug Thomas showed some promise
Neil Sachse Mick Nunan Geoff Motley Neil Kerley
Ken Eustice Stewie Palmer Glen Hewitt dontcha knew it
Craig Cock Adcock Woodcock any shlock
Malcolm Blight Bruce Light Ken Whelan how ya feelin?

Ya got -
Rex Voight Peter Woite Bob Hammond Kevin Salmon
Ian Day Elleway David Grainger there's a danger
Bob Quinn Trevor Sims Ian Brewer Ralph Sewer
Dave Boyd Daryl Hicks Sonny Morey that's the story
Robran Wigney Window Bagshaw
Lindsay Head Peter Marker Jeff Potter whatsa motter?

Came from Adelaide man, came from Adelaide man
South Australian made man, drank Woodies lemonade man
Shoulda been there when they played man
Came from Adelaide

Not Ballarat Bendigo Geelong Dandenong
Came from Adelaide

Port Club Song II

WORDS: Greg Champion–Jane Harris
TUNE: Port Power Club Song

When you grow up in Adelaide you learn young to hate Port. Just as it is with Melbourne's Magpies.

Time softens many things, and now many non-Port-following South Aussies are happy for them to beat anyone bar the Crows. Culturally stereotyping Port and its fans is close to my heart.

We've got our GTHOs
Our hot Monaros
Oh yeah, with hot-wired ignition
We've got our Monster Truck Shows
Our hate for the Crows
Oh yeah, Port Adelaide tradition

We've got souped-up Commodores
Cortinas of course
Oh yeah, with modified suspension
We've got rebuilt panel vans
Got Utes and Sandmans
Oh yeah, in as-new condition

We've got Pintaras with fats
We're covered in tatts
Oh yeah, you'll hear us when we're comin'
And we don't stop stop stop for the cop cop cops
Oh no, we know we can outrun 'em

If you want 180Bs
Or 120Ys
Oh yeah, we know about the caper
And we can do you a deal
For prices unreal
Complete, with full rego papers

When The Whistle Blows

Greg Champion [BMG publishing]

The return of the footy season has set many a pen to paper.

The leaves are blowing off the trees
And 'cross the avenue
The turning of the season's in the air
Something's gonna happen and
I know I have to go
And when the whistle blows I'll be there

This is why we come
This is what we know
I'll be there waiting when the whistle blows

We holidayed, we went away
We had our summer fun
The cricket fans have been and cheered and gone
Something else is stirring
Did I hear a distant cheer
And when the whistle blows I'll be here

This is why we come
This is what we know
I'll be there waiting when the whistle blows

And there's a venue near the heart of town
And that's where I have to go
to be there waiting when the whistle blows

The Story Of Fizzball McCann

Greg Champion [c.1988]

It was year nine in school, and our short story anthology was called *Southern Harvest*. The last tale in the book was *The Batting Wizard From The City*. A stranger wanders up to a bush cricket match and gets a game as they're one short. The ring-in ends up carving the hugely feared opposition bowler to all points of the compass. Comparisons are made with the great Victor Trumper. It wasn't until re-reading, much later, that I deduced that the unknown cricketer in the yarn *was* Trumper. While studying Australian Literature at Uni, I dug deeper into the tale's author: Dal Stivens. He wrote several charming books of such tales. That started a lifelong affection for Aussie sporting tall tales. This one is from 1988.

This is the story of the bowler
The bowler called Fizzball McCann
He bowled as fast as a runaway truck
Struck fear into every man

Chorus:
And it's three slips two gullies a cover
A short mid-off saving the one
It's a silly mid on and a backward square leg
As Fizzball McCann stats his run

Now Fizzball bowled fast, or he bowled 'em full length
But he'd never been known to bowl wide
and when he delivered the Fizzball
The batsmen just laid down and died

His eyes they bulge, his mouth it would quiver
His knees used to pound up and down
And when he delivered the Fizzball
a shudder went right 'round the ground

Repeat Chorus:
Now the annual game was against Patchewollock
Whose captain was the batsman named Gray
Reported by some to be the number one
Of all the best bats of his day

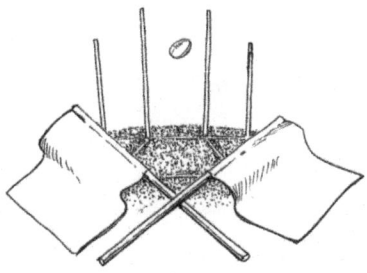

Well the match came around with the atmosphere heavy
The clouds were all gloomy and dark
The batting side trembled deep down in their boots
As Fizzball's men took to the park

Well the openers went quickly and cheaply
They were happy to get out alive
But Fizzball had his sights on the legendary bat
Who was due in down the order at five

Now the Captain named Gray had boasted to many
He'd hit Fizzball out of the ground
So when he took block at three down for twenty
Nobody uttered a sound

Repeat Chorus:
Well the ball left his hand with a whoosh and a roar
The batsman just stood there and stared
Middle and off stump shattered to pieces
The leg stump disappeared in thin air

Chorus:
And it's three slips two gullies a cover
A short mid-off saving the one
It's a silly mid on and a backward square leg
As Fizzball McCann stats his run

THE 2000s

In a wrenching move, The Coodabeens had switched from ABC to commercial radio in 1993. I voted against it and was not pleased, but I was only one voice. Circumstances made it near impossible to continue at the ABC at the time. We trundled along on 3AW, in my case, bumbled along...until I was contacted in 2002 by our dear ABC buddy and producer Rotten Ronnie, about a possible new program on ABC. One thing led to another and in 2003 the Coodabeen Champions were back on Dear Old Auntie. Our spiritual home. And there we have stayed, to this day.

At our *annual* (!!) production meeting before the 2003 season, where I always had very little to contribute, I lobbed up the notion that, with the rise of listeners' email ideas, I could arguably fill two ten-minute segments of songs, one segment per hour. I remember Cove giving me that withering look which implied: are you *sure* you can keep up the necessary broadcast standard for 20 minutes? And that's the way it's stayed until today. So from 2003 onward, ditty presentation became more factory-like. I'd search for good listener ideas to avoid having to think them up for myself; but I still cooked up my own songs too. Songs drifted to be less about individual players and more about lines, hooks, concepts that amused us. When *The Coodabeens* switched back from 3AW to the ABC, Tony elected to remain at 3AW. He'd carved out a significant niche for himself there. Of the original core team of five, this was our first line-up loss, after 20 years. Very early member and lifelong buddy of Ian Cover, Billy Baxter, was invited to re-join the team. One year later, founding member Simon, a QC, was appointed as the youngest ever Victorian Supreme Court judge. That made two core line-up losses in one year. But Torch was still with us on the footy show, having been there from near the start, so again the *Coodabeens* lumbered on. No further line-up changes to date.

← Singing with Coves at Kardinia Park, 2007, the day after the Cats won the flag. There were 30,000 in the stadium. Photo by Bernie Napthine

Members Of The MCC

WORDS: Greg Champion–John Ogge
TO THE TUNE OF: Born to Run

When John Ogge came up with this idea 15-20 years back, it quickly became the ultimate Members-teasing anthem. And the Members themselves— Lord love 'em—lovingly adopted it as their own 'club' song. It's probably one of the three most popular ditties since it all began in 1983.

By day we sit in the boardrooms of
our daddies' companies
At night we drive down Balwyn Road
in our four-wheel drive machines
Raised on Melway map fifty-nine
we grew up living on the right side of the tramlines – woh –
Baby my Volvo's got a roof rack
with the private school kiddies in the back
They go to Wesley and Haileybury
And baby blokes like us – we're members of the MCC

I keep the chains and the ski gear in the four-car garage
for the long weekends
I'm tossing up between a Lexus and a Merc
to go with my BM
Oh, baby it's been a long season
I might go insane if I don't escape to Dinner Plain – woh –
When we get through this financial year
if the Nasdaq's right I'm gonna
hit the slopes in France or Germany
And baby blokes like us we're members of the MCC

I'm gonna flash my medallion
meet the old man's friends
for a pre-game chardonnay
We're gonna shoot the breeze about securities
and find out who's playin' today
Oh baby I'm gettin' tired of all these jokers
who keep singing sarcastic songs about the Dees
And baby blokes like us – we're members of the MCC

Sheeds Is The Greatest

WORDS: Rhett Bartlett-Greg Champion
TO THE TUNE OF: The Greatest Love of All

Rhett is the son of KB, and is a keen listener to *The Coodabeens*.
He showed some top ditty skills when he sent in this idea.

I believe that Sheedy is the future
Pick him now and let him lead the team
Give him all the love he richly deserves
He's not really all that old
Just look at all those blokes in Chinese politics
They're all fair dinkum geriatrics

All this talk of who'll be Tigers coach
Buckley, Malthouse, Jim Jess, Michael Roach
Tony Free, Kent Kingsley or Mark Lee
Just give the gig to Sheeds, he is a genius
Name him although Caro
Says he's no good and, too old

He'll be great because we know
He'll bring back Martians and marshmallows
He'll wave his jacket in the air
And prove E doesn't equal MC squared
And on this point we can all trust
Sheedy is a genius

He is the greatest coach of all
And if it be God's plan
Who knows he might just get
KB back to Tigerland

We Are The Members

WORDS: Greg Champion–Peter Treseder
TO THE TUNE OF: Return to Sender

The MCC Members and Dees fans—these are the gifts that keep on giving, for so long. After a long time the jest started to wear thin—for some, but not for all.

I grew up in Malvern
I went to private school
My Daddy always told me
that we were born to rule – my Daddy told me

We are the members
and they are not!
So just remember
who's who and what's what!
We paid the money
for membership
and every winter we go
on our skiing trip

So we moved to Balwyn
then to Ivanhoe
But one thing never changed, though
the chalet in the snow – My Daddy told me –

We are the members
and at the game
You cheer a number
you don't cheer a name
Well done number 14!
Good luck number 2!
Chase hard there, new kid!
Roody doody do do

Club Songs Combined

WORDS: Greg Champion–Jane Harris–John Ogge–Stuart Macarthur
TO THE TUNE OF: Botany Bay

It's been said that most of the club songs have a dodgy line or two buried within.
I tried to pull together the best of them.

We're the admiration of a nation
we're respected by our foes
We hit 'em real high and we hit 'em low
and we give 'em the old heave-ho

Though they send us up we'll keep our end up
We're riding the bumps with a grin
If we are behind well, we never mind
'cos we're risking our head and our shin

Oh, ju-ust for rec-er-eation's sake
to pa-ass the ti-ime of day
we pla-ay the game as it should be played
at home or far away

Oh, what though the odds they be great or small
we shake down the thunder from the sky
Should old acquaintance be forgot
dawn to dark, still our banners fly high

We won't stop stop stop stop till we're top top top
'cos teamwork is the thing that talks
We have lots of fun we have heaps of fun
and the premiership is a cakewalk

Ballad Of Ben Cousins

WORDS: Greg Champion–Paul Chiodo
TO THE TUNE OF: The Highwayman

I have become teary singing this one, more than once. Circa 2008.

I was an air hostess
Across the country I did fly
Perth to Melbourne many times
Many a businessman responded to my smile
But only Ben could send me up a mile high
I still recall that certain crazed look in his eye
My feelings still survive

I was a constable
Just a copper on the beat
Met up with Ben once on the street
I pulled him up but he was way too quick for me
He swam the river and he hid among the reeds
They say he fell in with the wrong sort of crowd
I'll miss him anyhow

I was a tabloid hack
I was camped at Benny's place
I wrote of downfall and disgrace
I staked out nightclubs when he went out on the town
We wrote the headlines that helped to bring him down
Is football better off now that he's been kicked out
I still have my doubts

I was a grandmother
Followed West Coast all those years
Ben held the Cup, I shed a tear
I don't know much about what young folk do these days
I only know the thrill he gave us when he played
I want to tell him that I understand his pain
I hope he plays again

Dees, The Melbourne Club

WORDS: John Ogge–Greg Champion
TO THE TUNE OF: Do Re Mi

From 2004, a time when the Dees and Members and snow gags all rolled easily into one.

Dees – our team, the Melbourne club
Row – I used to do at school
'G – a place to park my car
Car – my BM double U
So – long since we won the Cup
Four-ty years I'd given up
Ski – what we do when we lose
Are you Dees' supporters too?

A pre-dinner chardonnay
Be an upright citizen
See the sights of Dinner Plain
Dees – I sometimes follow them
O, we own expensive land
Pe-ter works for his old man
Queue, we members never do
Are you Dees' supporters too?

P – Prince Alfred Younger set
G can only mean gluwein
N is for the great Norm Smith
Al – so well done number nine
S it stands for St Mauritz
H it must be Hassa Mann
M – I have a membership
And C's for chalet-owned-by-the-old-man

Chapel Street Nightclub, Two AM Shopfront Incident

WORDS: Greg Champion–Noel Dennison
TO THE TUNE OF: Folsom Prison Blues

The famous Sunday morning two AM Prahran shopfront affair. The Boy from Upper Beaconsfield has been very tolerant of the many songs about him. When it comes to footy songs, Brendan is the gift that keeps on giving.

Security's a-comin'
and I think I know why
I'd better get a wriggle on
but I can't do up my fly
I hope it's not on video
that would be the end
I was only tryin' to shake hands
with the wife's best friend

When I was just a young man
my old man told me boy
Be careful where you shake hands
with the unemployed
But horses must be watered
potatoes must be strained
Percy must be pointed
at the porcelain

I know I got it comin'
I made a big mistake
Next time I'll take a look around
before I shake the snake
This time the club has told me
they're gonna throw me out
I was only tryin' to go where –
where the big knobs hang out

Get Tommy Back To Richmond

Greg Champion [BMG Publishing]

Throughout the Noughties the Tigers struggled. A common term tossed up, perhaps tongue-in-cheek—but not always—was to get Tommy Hafey back to Punt Road.

Stop changin' the rules, bring the Seconds back
Get rid of the chip game, bring the prices down
Get rid of the advantage to Interstate clubs
And bring back kick to kick after the siren

Yes – and get Tommy back to Richmond

Down with barcode turnstiles
and four-dollar buckets of chips
Down with City Hall and the powers-that-be
and ivory towers, and down with biased umpires
Get rid of the twilight Sunday games

And stop muckin' around, get Tommy back to Richmond

Ban clash jumper away strip rubbish
simplify the draft
And make the Eagles, Port and Dockers
have to come up with new club songs
or they won't be allowed back into football

Bring back The Winners, League Teams
and Footy Replay
How 'bout 6 games on a Saturday

Yes – and get Tommy back to Richmond

Let the public into the
private levels at Docklands
Make the Footy Show go away
and will Patrick Smith ever stop baggin' Andre?

Don't change any more rules
even if they're improvements
And how 'bout five or even four games on a Saturday

Get Tommy back to Richmond

Henley Beach Hotel Incident

WORDS: Greg Champion
TO THE TUNE OF: Battle of New Orleans

In an incident that still amuses *The Coodabeens* to this day, legend has it that players of the two Adelaide AFL teams met at a pub for an off-field 'Showdown'. As I hail from this town (West Horsham) I follow one of these two sides, and it's not Port.

In 1836 they built a little town
They said this'll be the spot for a showdown
One'll be Port and one'll be the Crows
And they can battle it out until the cows come home

Two hundred years later and the showdowns were hot
And just after Port had won four on the trot
They all adjourned to a watering hole
And proceeded to act like the convicts of old

They drank their drinks and the players kept arriving
Down from Tapleys Hill and West Beach Road
'Cos word got out that a hotel carpark
was where the two tribes were gonna have a go

They all assembled near the beach that day
To settle their differences the old-fashioned way
Nothing too rough, just a push and a shove
Just to reflect their respect and love

One pushed one and one pushed the other
And before you knew it, it was really on
The cops were called but before they got there
The pub was empty and the players were gone

And over at West Lakes and down at the Port
They chuckled and said "it was just a bit of sport
That's the way the game should be played
And that's how we do things in old Adelaide"

They drank their drinks and the players kept arriving
Down from Tapleys Hill and West Beach Road
One pushed one and one pushed the other
And before you knew it they were having a go

One Tony Lockett

WORDS: Greg Champion
TO THE TUNE OF: Guantanamera

I believe that Sydney fans used to chant this chorus at the ground. James Freud had a hit using that chorus. On *The Coodabeens* we steered it another way, in 1998.

One Tony Lockett
there's only one Tony Lockett
One Tony Lockett
there's only one Tony Lockett

I wear the red Sydney Swans pants
Some say I've had a hair transplant
I am one beefy hombrero
And I enjoy the pleasures of the souvlaki
They have the power to delight and inspire me

One Tony Lockett
there's only one Tony Lockett
One Tony Lockett
there's only one Tony Lockett

yo soy un hombre di multo kilogrammo
di multo enchilada e tortilla e burrito
yo soy grando conquistadore

the words say:
I am a simple man from the forested Central Highlands
of a major Southern State
and before I leave this world
I want to share my gift for goalkicking
all thirteen hundred of them
My goals are soft green
but they are also flaming crimson
With the poor people of this Earth
I want to share my goals
The little goals from the snap and the pockets
Please me more than the set shots
One Tony Lockett
there's only one Tony Lockett
One Tony Lockett
there's only one Tony Lockett

The Day Mick Malthouse Smiled

WORDS: Greg Champion–Richard Evans
TO THE TUNE OF: American Pie

This tune has been a favourite for listeners, and understandably: It's an epic and classic of the era.

Quite a long while ago
I recall a young Mick Malthouse at the Tiges
He may not have had much dash
but he had a pretty fair moustache
and he was kinda medium for his size

But as a coach he became a scowler
a grumpy groucher and a growler
Even after big wins, he never raised a faint grin
So footy fans they nearly cried
when Maggies beat the Sydney side
We all felt it deep inside, the day, Mick Malthouse, smiled

The fans were singing, my, my did you see Micky smile?
They reckon he last did it as a four-year-old child
Was that one of the Shaw boys, drinking whisky & rye
Now – can we win a game in July
Will we ever win a game in July

Now for ten years he's been out to get
a flag down there but no luck yet
We've had some laughs along the way
like when the jester there behind the goals
donned the jacket made of gold
and gave us all a smile on Anzac Day

You tell us what we need to know
like why the ox is always slow
and the earth is always round
Yeah, we all wrote that one down
and the three men we admire most
Buckley, Voss and goodness knows
All applied to coach Gold Coast
the day Mick Malthouse smiled

My Son Likes The Tigers

WORDS: Leigh Schneider–Greg Champion
TO THE TUNE OF: Delilah

The time-honoured topic of the shame of raising a son who decides not to follow the Dees.

My son was home-birthed in our holiday house in Sorrento
I bought him his Melbourne membership pack right away
He went to Auskick
Nobody told me that Richmond was hosting that day

My son likes the Tigers. Why oh why the Tigers
He's, off the Dees, he's embarrassed the whole family
How can I face all the chaps down at the MCC

He's given up his Range Rover and Hugo Boss jacket
He's wearing moccies and he wants to get a tattoo
He stands in the outer
He reads Inside Football and not the Financial Review

My son likes the Tigers. Why oh why the Tigers
Oh, the pain. He drinks cleanskins instead of Grange
It's all been too much for the poor lads down at the Exchange

Refrain:
He takes public transport
He's turned down Klosters to go skiing at Dinner Plain

My son likes the Tigers. Why oh why the Tigers
Grammar's told me, he's more suited to Haileybury
He's out of the will 'cause he just will not follow the Dees!

Kick 'Em When They're Down

WORDS: Greg Champion
TO THE TUNE OF: Ruby, don't take your love to town

Just as well for me that 99+ per cent of Collingwood fans take this stuff in good humour. I've had only one or two scrapes with Pie fans and that's not bad in more than thirty years. Anything for a laugh, is my defence. Pie fans have let me off very lightly. Now, Hawks fans on the other hand…

It's not nice to see a mighty club, driven to its knees
We shouldn't laugh if certain teams are low on victories
There's more than one disappointing footy club in town
But Collingwood – ya gotta kick 'em when they're down

Some may say that Carlton's had its share of tragedy
You might wanna argue Carlton's earnt some sympathy
But be that as it may there's only one real game in town
Oh Maggies – ya gotta kick 'em when they're down

The Bombers aren't so popular, they get on people's nerves
Others reckon Hawthorn's getting all that it deserves
While there's not a lotta haters of the Dogs and Cats around
But black and white – ya gotta kick 'em when they're down

Manuka Oval

WORDS: Greg Champion
TO THE TUNE OF: Dancing in the Dark

The national capital's charms could inspire anyone to song. A rich wonderland of delight.

I'm driving Northbourne Avenue
I see Botanical Gardens everywhere
I'm on my way through Civic
There's a big game on and I gotta be there
I'm not talkin' 'bout pollies
Not Labour v Liberal or any of that
Talkin' AFL here
Today Canberra hosts a big big match

See that metal spire
Top o' Parliament House, well that's so ho hum
Crossin' Lake Burley-Griffin
Look out, Manuka Oval here I come

Around Capital Circle
Just ignore the sign to Kingston Shops
Exit at Canberra Avenue
Powerin' on to Griffith and we're not gonna stop
If you end up in Fyshwick
If you end up in Fyshwick you've gone too far
Take Captain Cook Crescent
And before you know it there you are

It's nowhere near Woden
Or Downer or Dickson or Deakin, no way
It's Manuka Oval
Kangaroos and Crowboys come to play

It's not called *Manooka*
If you say *Manooka* you'd be wrong
Kangaroos and Crowboys
Yeah come on baby, we're going along

Swans Club Song II

WORDS: Greg Champion
TO THE TUNE OF: Swans Club song

From the nineties when it was still felt that much of Sydney didn't know—or care—much about the Swans.

Oh how Sydney just loves the Swans
They just adore that aerial ping pong
The best thing to happen to Sydney by far
Since the monorail and the Gay Mardi Gras

Down at the Rocks and Wooloomooloo
they all discuss the Barry Hall news
and raise their glass of Tooheys high
and cheer, cheer the red and white

In the cafes of Ryde and Rose Bay
they talk about Darryn Cresswell all day
everybody wears Swans regalia
in the most exciting town in Australia

Be it Dee Why or be it Crows Nest
they all agree the Swans are the best
From Darlinghurst down to Kings Cross
they're hoping to catch a glimpse of Wayne Schwass

Cheer, cheer the Swans of Sydney
they've got the town in a footy frenzy
and they'll party till the Centre Point Tower comes down
when the Swans bring the flag to town

The Scary Pharmacist

Greg Champion [BMG publishing]

Not naming any names here, but if you were to look in the direction of the Bombers' coaching box...I think the term 'the late arriver' may have been coined for this citizen.

Now in a corner of Western Australia
There is a pharmacy
And in that pharmacy's a man
Who's nice as he can be

And he hands out the cough medicine
And he dishes out the Calamine
And he handles your prescriptions
And he helps people all the time

And between Monday and Friday
He's always meek and mild
But on weekends he becomes a
Schizoid monster running wild

And his head turns into concrete
And his body doubles in size
And hair grows all over his back
And there's a glazed look in his eyes

And he heads for the West Coast Eagles game
And he slips in through the gate
But he can't seem to get to the game on time
'cos he's always arriving late

And like Superman he removes his specs
And he puffs out his barrel chest
And when he pops number 24 on his back
He's the Bogey Man of the West

Then Monday morning he's back dispensing
Prescriptions for panadeine
And he's the nicest sweetest charmingest
Pharmacist you've ever seen

But something's not quite right with him
Because when he goes out to lunch
He charges the light poles on the street
And he hits 'em with a mighty crunch

Crows Club Song

WORDS: Greg Champion–Jane Harris
TO THE TUNE OF: Crows Club Song

The Crows and their fans do not escape stereotyping. Being from South Australia, I leave it to the other *Coodabeens* to poke the fun. They sure like to have a crack at the wine drinking, and alleged artistic inclinations of South Australians.

We were going to go to West Lakes
but Wilpena's looking good
We had tickets for the showdown
but we've always thought we should
take a cruise along the Coorong
Stop and see Mount Gambier
and I've heard there's a confronting play
at the Festival Theat-re

We've been going to take the caravan
'cross to Eyre Peninsula
We could come back through the Flinders
hey, it's really not that far
While the Crows are struggling, why don't we
go to Kangaroo Isl-and?
Yes, and Hahndorf's underrated
we could pop up this weekend

We could do our favourite galleries
on the drive down to Vict-a
And apparently the wineries
have improved around Gool-wa
Let Neil Craig rejig our game plan
I've run low on cab-merlots
There is more to South Australia
Than the silly old Adelaide Crows

When The Pies Tumble Down In July

WORDS: Greg Champion–Jane Harris
TO THE TUNE OF: When The Rain Tumbles Down in July (Traditional owner: Slim Dusty)

Through the nineties and noughties, the Magpies began with a rush… then came July.

There's a sombre mood in the changeroom
the lockers stand lonely and bare
There's a cloud hanging over The Chairman
who would want to be a millionaire
Angry coach glares at the press conference
the daggers they flash from his eyes
Yeah but that's just the old Magpie story
When the Pies tumble down in July

In the paper Mike Sheahan is probing
Chris Tarrant and Rocca are named
As Mick gives another press conference
and refuses to lay any blame
And the fans and the cheer squad look angry
They scream that they've been crucified
Ah, but that's just what happens each winter
When the Pies tumble down in July

There are things that are constant in football
like Grant Thomas baffling us all
Like KB not talking to Richmond
Criticising the tribun-al
There's a look on the face of The Chairman
The sponsors stand nervously by
It's a time-honoured football tradition
that the Pies tumble down in July

Yeah, and that's just the old Magpie story
When the Pies tumble down in July

Down To The Torrens

WORDS: Chris McDonough–Greg Champion
TO THE TUNE OF: The river

Pardon the stereotyping, Port fans. Anything for a chuckle. Since I was a guest of President Brian Cunningham at a Port lunch, I've grown out of any Port antipathy. Like plenty of non-Port South Australians, I like to see them do well. Though, not all South Aussies do.

I come from down Port Adelaide
Where they teach you when you're young
about the white goods industry
and how certain things are done
When Ports went and joined that AFL
I was still a crime-free child
When they won that flag back in 0-four
my whole cell block went wild

I got a good job when I got out
just fixing up people's cars
I was switching plates and turning back speedos
in a Woodville caryard
And on my 30th birthday
I got me a Power tattoo
We celebrated at Pooraka Hotel
where I found me a new car too

And we'd go down to the Torrens
up near that new footbridge
Yeah, to pick up a brand new two door fridge

Now youse umpires, ya better watch out
'Cos we know youse hate us all
Youse report us for head high contact, when
we're only tryin' to punch the ball
Youse never pay us any free kicks
those Crows get every free you give
but we know where you park your car
and we can find out where you live

Your car could go down to the Torrens
Minus wheels and the stereo
'Neath the black Torrens water it could go

Favourite Things

WORDS: Greg Champion–Jane Harris–John Ogge
TO THE TUNE OF: My Favourite Things

The stereotyping rolls on. Mercifully the vast majority of Dees fans and the MCC Members are amused.

Warm corporate boxes where no-one needs mittens
Late model Rollers we got for a pittance
Off-road Range Rovers that never have dings
These are a Demon fan's favourite things

Nice young snow bunnies at après ski bashes
Instructors called Helmut with trendy moustaches
Discussing why Mark Jamar's so interesting
These are a Demon fan's favourite things

Melbourne Cup marquees and chalets at Klosters
Expressing disgust at that bloke who ran Foster's
Knowing that Robbie Flower played on a wing
These are a Demon fan's favourite things

When the Dees lose, when it's bad news
When we're thrashed again
We simply remember our favourite things
And then we buy more of them

Down To Kardinia

WORDS: Greg Champion–Alf Davies–John Ogge
TO THE TUNE OF: The River

A wander through the Geelong of yesteryear.

I come from down Corio, where mister when you're young
They bring you up to think you'll be another Neville Bruns
I grew up with the Nankervis boys in the back streets of Anakie
And there wasn't a lot to cheer about, around 1963

We'd go down to Kardinia and cheer our side with pride
When the Nankervis boys would kick it wi-i-de

We lost in '67 and we took it pretty hard
But for my 19th birthday I got a Michael Turner Scanlan's footy card
I took it to school and swapped it for a Scratcher Neal card, but then
Someone beat me up and flogged it and I never got it back again

We'd go down to Kardinia with a thermos of mum's best soup
Oh, and cheer for the blue and white hoops

We got into a few Grand Finals in those dark and cruel nineties
But lately there ain't been much success on account of the conspiracy
The draw is stacked against us we always play the stronger teams
And the AFL makes sure we don't get seen on TV

But I've seen Gary Malarkey and Bobby Davis
I saw Sidey waving at the Waverley bus
And at nights in Norlane I lie awake
And replay all the marks I saw Ablett take
Now those memories come back to haunt me
They haunt me like a curse
Missing out on those Grand Finals, well
What could ever be worse

And we'd go down to Kardinia and through the old-fashioned turnstiles
Oh, and after, get sloshed at the Lord of the Isles

The Power And The Crow

WORDS: Greg Champion
TO THE TUNE OF: The Orange and the Green

A dip into the underbelly of football culture in Adelaide.
Some of this is pretty close to home for me.

Oh, it is the biggest mix-up that you have ever known
Me father is a Power man, me mother she's a Crow

Oh my Daddy is blue collar, from Ethelton came he
My mother is a Beaumont girl she went to MLC
At a motel in Glenelg the two were wed and honeymooned
But since Port joined the AFL they sleep in separate rooms

Oh, and when the Crows arrived my mother fell for Nigel Smart
Scotty Hodges, David Marshall, cute young Benny Hart
While Daddy fed me stories of Alberton by night
And raved about his heroes David Grainger and Bruce Light

Oh, it is the biggest mix-up that you have ever known
Me father is a Power man, me mother she's a Crow

When I was small my Mum said, "if you know what's good for you
You'll be a loyal Norwood boy and dress in red and blue"
But me Dad had other plans, as soon as Mum was out of sight
He'd dress me in the prison stripes of Magpie black and white

Then one day at Football Park it was at Showdown X One Vee
I was with me Mum and Dad when things began to turn ug-ly
Pretty soon it fired up, a Ramsgate-style melee
And me bein' strictly neutral everybody belted me

Oh, it is the biggest mix-up that you have ever known
Me father is a Power man, me mother she's a Crow

Go Go Youse Kiwis

Greg Champion [BMG publishing]

The Kiwis won something bug—it might have been the Rugby World Cup—but they're always winning that. It wasn't the America's Cup—that was too long ago—but it was sumthung bug! And it warranted them being congretchalated. The song rocks hard, so I optimistically sent it to six NZ radio stations. Not a squeak.

Go go youse Kiwis
Youse were sinsational
Go go youse Kiwis
Youse were turrufuc
Go go youse Kiwis
Youse were megnufucent
Youse mighty Kiwis
How good was thet!

Go go youse Kiwis
Youse were lidjundary
Go go youse Kiwis
youse were stupindus
Go go youse Kiwis
Youse played trumindus
Youse mighty Kiwis
How good was thet!

You kipt us fessunated
we were igg-zularated
Should be congretchalated
For what you dud
You made the world sut up
end pay attinshun
Youse mighty Kiwis
youse are the bist !

Cricket's On The Radio

Greg Champion [BMG publishing]

I've learnt that many Aussies relate to this feeling: a mid-summer day, you're on hols, there's a Test or a one-dayer on, and ABC radio becomes your chief companion.

But there's another key thing to this reverie: it's the *pace* of the commentary that's critical. Take a bow Jim Maxwell, Drew Morphett [sadly missed], Alan McGilivray, Tim Lane, Neville Oliver and all the British orator doyens: Brian Johnston, John Arlott, Christopher Martin-Jenkins. It was the smoooothness, the relaxation, the tone, that sooothed you, the listener. Cricket callers must soooth. They must not hurry. Cricket is not a horse race or a footy game in terms of commentating—it's an all-day affair.

The star callers talked at the pace of an Aussie summer's day.

Life is lazy, life is sweet when January comes
As long as one team's bowling and the other's making runs
I know as soon as I wake up if it's my lucky day
If the cricket's on the ABC then everything's okay

And the cricket's on the radio
And everybody's laying low
Just the cricket on the radio
And nowhere that I have to go

Draw the curtains pull the blinds, it's beating down out there
Pop the feet up daddy, there is cricket on the air
I love the sleepy rhythm of the commentators' call
Just the ABC and me and I'll hang on every ball

And the cricket's on the radio
And everybody's laying low
Just the cricket on the radio
And nowhere that I have to go

And there's nothing that I have to do
Nowhere I have to go
So roll that wicket, I've got cricket on my radio

And the cricket's on the radio
And everybody's laying low
Just the cricket on the radio
On the radio

Ballad Of Andrew McLeod

WORDS: Greg Champion–Greg Loechel
TO THE TUNE OF: Old Dogs and Children and Watermelon Wine

The other *Coodabeens* love to reinforce the stereotype of Adelaide being full of arty, street-poet types. And as for Crows fans, it's been a pretty fair 27 years: Nigel Smart, Tony Modra, Ben Hart, Mark Bickley, Mark Ricciuto, Tyson Edwards, Shaun Rehn, the Jarmans, Andrew and Darren, Simon Goodwin, and, of course, Andrew McLeod—plenty to smile about.

Who's the best Crow you have seen
the Old Thespian said to me
He said "I'd like to put my case
for number twenty-three"
I was in a bar in Gouger Street
A jazz band playing loud
When the Thespian he chewed my ear
About Andrew McLeod

There were hardly any punters but
this street artist and me
His resemblance to Don Dunstan was
truly uncanny
Uninvited he sat down
and told me just how proud
he was of Goodwin, Edwards
Ricciuto and McLeod

Edwards came from Westies
and before that Tailem Bend
Goodwin was a Panther
and a giant among men
Ricciuto a Colossus
a standout in the crowd
But the Thespian waxed lyrical
About Andrew Mcleod

I had to leave to catch a tram
along King William Street
The street performer warming up
about Eddie Hocking's feats
That night I dreamed of taking
Modra speccies in the clouds
with the Edwardses and Goodwins
Ricciutos and McLeods

Gavin Wanganeen

WORDS: Greg Champion–John Ogge
TO THE TUNE OF: Vincent

Gavin Wanganeen was one of those players about whom it was said: "you can't touch him!!"
He did seem to get a very cosy run with the umps. Not knocking his giftedness, though.

Gavin Wanganeen
what a crazy ride it's been
Brownlow medal at nineteen
A flag the same year, every schoolboy's dream

Transferred at twenty-two
To the black and white and blue
The injuries you've struggled through
And Brownlow number two now beckons you

I don't understand
How you get the frees you do
Why the umpires are so soft on you
Is it your eyes of china blue?
No-one's ever found the reason yet
For all the frees you get

And another mystery
is how you never give away the free
Is there some conspiracy
Or do the umps see something we don't see?

For they cannot touch you
We know this to be true
For when no-one was there to handball to
one starry West Lakes night
You held the ball as others often do
But I could have told you Gavin
No umpire in the world would raise his whistle against you

Coach The Dees

WORDS: Greg Champion–John Ogge
TO THE TUNE OF: Catch the Wind

In the chilly months of winter
When I should be up at Crackenback
Trying out my new expensive skis

I dream of ending poverty
And the hope of peace in the Middle East
Ah, but I may as well try and coach the Dees

When it's two-foot-deep at Dinner Plain
And David Neitz is playing in pain
And Russell Roberston don't get no frees

I worry about old KB's feud
And about Chris Tarrant's attitude
Ah, but I may as well try and coach the Dees

When I'm popping down to town again
To do some business for the old man
And the radio says Dees are on their knees

And I fret about Fevola's mind
And if Ben Cousins has served his time
Ah, but I may as well try and coach the Dees

Put The Whistle Away

WORDS: Greg Champion
TO THE TUNE OF: House of the Rising Sun

The title is one of the many rich, historic phrases in the footy lexicon.
There are certain frees—in finals mostly—that haunt us all.

It's a game of many moments
Of magic and mystique
Of brilliant skills, and thrills that help
To make our code unique

And year by year our sport evolves
It never stays the same
That's why the rules committee's there
To keep pace with the game

Now certain things are sacred
Like the singing of club songs
And how the umps conduct themselves
Deep into time on

And should a match be up for grabs
With minutes left to play
There's one time-honoured traditional law
You put the whistle away

Just put the whistle away me lads
It's always been that way
The law's come down through centuries
put the whistle away

What happened 'tween the Saints & Cats
the 'Pies & Adelaide
are abominations to history
Ye must put the whistle away

FROM 2010

Our much-loved producer of about 15 years, Rotten Ronnie Engelhardt [LMCT6574, as the gag goes], was thinking of hanging up the headphones. A 20-year-old chap had approached him about sitting in and helping out. 'Young' Andy Bellairs, who'd grown up in the bush listening to us, spent about a year sitting next to Ron and, bingo!—he's been with us ever since. And, he's become a critical part of the team for the past 13 years. I estimate the number of ditties that have gone to air in my thirty-five years on the show at more than 4000. We've even collated a list of the 100 most-used tunes. I feel sure that I'm only reaching my best form now, with this odd caper. I believe I can keep improving at it.

← During the making of the 2013 video for the song *Mercy Lord Where is the Melody*. The song was a cynical shot at certain tuneless country songs. One country community broadcaster told me later: "I just couldn't work out what the song was about". Understandably...the song only got half way up the country chart. Photo by Ange Champion

Could've Almost Won The Flag

WORDS: Greg Champion
TO THE TUNE OF: Always on my Mind

This title became a running gag on *The Coodabeens* radio show. Crows in '93. Doggies in '97-'98. And so on.

Once the Magpies looked world beaters
It was back about round five
But when Scotty Burns got injured
Premiership hopes took a dive
What a dreadful blow for Collingwood
Just when things were looking good
Could've almost won the flag
Could've almost won the flag

Now let's turn back the time clock
1985's the year
the artists now called Western Bulldogs
were about to hit top gear
but for losing the Preliminary
16.13 to 15.9
they were going to win the flag
But they didn't win the flag

Tell me tell me all about the ones that got away
Give me, one more chance to have it end a different way
end a different way

Now it's early in the Nineties
it's a big preliminary
and a team in their third season
is forty-two points in the lead
Andrew Jarman takes a set shot
From just 15 metres out...
Could've almost won the flag
Could've almost won the flag

Everybody Slips At The Dome

WORDS: Greg Champion–Jane Harris–John Ogge
TO THE TUNE OF: Rainy Day Women

Jane Harris has been a provider of top song ideas for 15-20 years. Docklands endured years with a suspect surface. A high point for this song was at our annual Melbourne Arts Centre concert. A boy who was about twelve years old came out of the audience and sang the whole thing, unaccompanied.

Well you'll slip when you're playin' at the dome
You'll be out on a wing and all alone
You'll be waving to your teammate for the ball
And you'll fall down for no reason at all
It's the slipperiest surface ever grown
Everybody slips at the Dome

Well you'll slip when there's no way you think you will
Slip even when you're standing still
Slip just as you go to handpass
Your eyes'll slip just looking at the grass
University tests have clearly shown
Everybody slips at the Dome

Well you'll slip when you're on the boundary line
In the huddle at three-quarter time
Slip as you're jogging down the race
Fall and go splat upon your face
Even if you're sittin' in the stands
Everybody slips at Docklands

Well you'll slip as you're getting off the train
Slip even when it hasn't rained
Slip when you're standing in the queue
And spill tomato sauce all over you
But don't feel so bad, you're not alone
Everybody slips at the Dome

We Finished Ninth Again

WORDS: Greg Champion
TO THE TUNE OF: Richmond Club song

One of the perennial running gags of footy; well until 2017 at least, was the Tigers finishing ninth. And this is one of our most liked songs. It's only forty seconds long. There are three YouTube versions that have been created by people we don't know of, with 398,000 views.

We finished ninth again
The Richmond Tigers finished ninth again
In any season you will see it is our fate
to miss out on the eight
We win a few and lose a lot and then it is too late

We just went down the drain
We've never been much good since 1982
Be it Frawley or Jewell, Northey or Giesch
We win a few late, and just miss the eight
We finished ninth again

We've Won The Wooden Spoon

WORDS: Peter Otzen–Greg Champion–Moss
TO THE TUNE OF: Carlton Club Song

I think it was Peter Otzen, a *Coodabeens* listener, who came up with the ripper fork/kitchenware/salad set theme.

We've won the wooden spoon
We've got the good old wooden spoon
Wooden spoon we've lined it up since June
It's the wooden spoon that we'll win soon

Fans used to jeer us
They used to fear us
But now the sneer at us
'Cos now it's twice that we've gone bottom
We've got the good old wooden spoon

We've got the wooden spoon
We've got a lovely wooden spoon
And, next year, in spite of all the talk
We won't win the spoon we'll win the fork

And then the next year
While we're still down there
We'll get more kitchenware
Then it's the wooden bowl that we'll get
To have a lovely salad set

The Daniher Clan

WORDS: Greg Champion
TO THE TUNE OF: The Beverly Hillbillies

Written at the request of Neale and Bernard, for a tribute event. Bernard said Neale's directions were: absolutely nothing sad, light-heartedness only. A little research revealed much: The Daniher grandfather, and Catholicism, drove the growth of the clan and of Ungarie from the 1920s.

This here's the story of the Daniher folk
Seven lovely girls and four crazy blokes
From the back country of Ungarie
Where Jim met Edna and created history

Now Terry was the eldest and, wackiest as well
He could make a crowd laugh like ringin' a bell
At Wagga Tigers, five flags in six years
And legend has it he doesn't mind a beer

Now Neale was the third kid and, boy could he play
Better than himself, at the very same age
Captained the Bombers, played state of origin
His knees packed up at age of twenty-one

Now Chris and Anthony soon came along
And before ya know it they're all at Essendon
Together the four achieved something never seen
All four brothers picked in one State team

Now the drive to Ungarie is far and it's long
And the Big Smoke for them means West Wyalong
And Grandad Daniher in 1923
Helped build the Catholic church – they're as Catholic as can be

Now Jim Daniher's Dad was called Jim too
And when Jim married Edna all hell broke loose
They figured on five kids, six maybe seven
And blow me down, if they didn't have eleven

This here's the story of the Daniher crowd
Eleven kids that made Jim & Edna proud
If you're lookin' for Danihers, then start your search
At Saint Joe's Ungarie Catholic Church

Train To Montmorency

WORDS: Greg Champion
TO THE TUNE OF: City of New Orleans

This, along with *Members of the MCC*, may be the two most fondly-regarded footy songs over the whole journey. The suburb of Montmorency—very near where I live these days—has caused plenty of amusement with *The Coodabeens*, especially as every quiz caller from Monty invariably barracks for the Pies. The Hurstbridge line train carrying Pies fans became a topic of much jesting for *The Coodabeens*, and eventually this ditty ensued.

Ridin' on the train from Montmorency
black and white as far as the eye can see
Pass the paper bag that holds the bottle
Bound for Friday football at the 'G
And the sons of railway workers
And the mums of Union members
And they pick up more at Greensborough and Macleod
And they all join in that worn refrain
About upholding the Magpie name
And too bad if you're not one of the crowd

Here comes the 6.15 from Hurstbridge
Ferrying the feral Magpie hordes
It's the black and white express from Montmorency
And if you're not one of them don't get on board

Before it even gets to Montmorency
it stops at Wattle Glen and Diamond Creek
even scrapes a few folk up at Eltham
this will be the highlight of their week
And from Alphington down to Fairfield
from Heidelberg to Clifton Hill
but none from Eaglemont or Ivanhoe
Stopping at Victoria Park as evening fades away to dark
They talk about why Malthouse had to go

Night time on the train to Montmorency
all forlorn now, such a quiet ride
Didn't turn out quite how they expected
and once again completely crucified
As they roll through dirty Richmond
and on through Westgarth Station
they talk of other things to hide their grief
And mostly their discussion turns
to everybody's chief concern, and that's
how to get a better set of teeth

There goes the 10.15 to Hurstbridge
Ferrying the feral Magpie hordes
It's the black and white express to Montmorency
And if you're not one of them don't get on board

The Dees Have A Bye

WORDS: Greg Champion–Noel Dennison
TO THE TUNE OF: The Sounds of Goodbye

It's not a Kamahl hit that I remember—so I had to YouTube it—and I'm glad I did, because Noel's idea has become a big favourite with both *The Coodabeens* and with the Members when we sing it in the Members' Dining Room.

The swirling wind is sweeping leaves around the concourse of the MCG
It's one pm on Saturday I'm wondering: where could all the members be?
The long weekend in June is clearly many weeks away
So the call of the snow cannot be why
Then I recall some story in the papers

The Dees have a bye, the Dees have a bye

The long room leather lounges sit deserted, today no Members meet
Along the many lonely rows no tartan rugs laid out reserving seats
I might just drive the Beemer out to Sunbury
And watch Rupertswood take on Melbourne High
I just don't feel I fit in well at Casey

When the Dees have a bye, the Dees have a bye

A notice says no Saturday afternoon games here until round fourteen
Yet hark, I hear the cries of phantom crowds from past encounters here there've been
And through the mists I see the throng streaming through the park
And this eerie quiet's hard to justify
It's two o'clock on Saturday in Melbourne

And The Dees have a bye, the Dees have a bye

Just Like A Dermott Brereton

Greg Champion [BMG publishing]

She won the first AFLW best and fairest medal, in 2017. When Erin Phillips returned from injury in season 2018, she kicked four of her team's six goals that day. A 'handy' player.

Just like a Dermott Brereton
She was dominating the park
An old-fashioned centre-half-forward
Taking big contested marks

I watched the Crows and the Bulldogs
At the fine old Norwood ground
Erin was back in the line-up
And she made it clear she wasn't messing around
Snappin' 'em from the pocket
Soccering out of the air
The Bulldogs looked like they had it sewn up but
Lauren had other ideas

Just like a Dermott Brereton
That's how she takes the game on
An old-fashioned centre-half-forward
All in a zone, a zone of her own
Just like a Dermott Brereton
She was dominating the park
An old-fashioned centre-half-forward
Taking big contested marks

She'd been out with injury
For the side, there was plenty at stake
She ran out with a mission, oh yes
She had a statement, a statement to make

Just like a Dermott Brereton
That's how she takes the game on
An old-fashioned centre-half-forward
All in a zone, a zone of her own
Just like a Dermott Brereton
She was dominating the park
An old-fashioned centre-half-forward
Taking big contested marks

Big contested, big contested
Big contested marks

Camera On The Wing

WORDS: Greg Champion–Richard Evans
TO THE TUNE OF: Home Among the Gumtrees
TRADITIONAL OWNERS: Bob Brown and Wally Johnson

Perhaps this is my number one soapbox: watching footy on TV and you lose the thread of play due to the needless switching of camera angles. Often, game action is missed due to multiple slow-mo replays of—nothin'! If it ain't broke—break it.

We've watched a lotta footy now
over many years
Jezza's mark & Gabbo's run
we've shared the thrills and tears
And everything we witnessed
for many decades past
from a camera on the wing, so come on

Just put a camera on the wing mate
For heaven's sake mate
just put it there and leave it there
And none behind the goals
or on the boundary line
'cos it just stuffs up the game

Saw Ablett taking screamers
and Lethal break the post
Barassi in the huddle
the exploits of The Ghost
And never did the camera need to jump around
'cos it just stuffs up the game, fair dinkum

Just put a camera on the wing mate
for heaven's sake mate
Just put it there and leave it there
and none behind the goals
or on the boundary line
'cos it just stuffs up the game

'Cos it just – stuffs – up – the – game!

From Whence It Came

WORDS: Greg Champion
TUNE SUGGESTION: Patti from Reservoir
TO THE TUNE OF: Forever Young

A firm fave for me. When we've sung it to the crowd at the MCG on Grand Final day, it's uplifting. I think Richard Evans identified the phrase—a common expression of commentators from the old days—as good for a song. Our email group tossed around a number of tunes and Patti from Rezza suggested this one.

I still hear the golden voices
Doug Heywood's soothing sound
the smoothness of Clarke Hansen
Geoff Leek, around the grounds
Doug Bigelow's church football
They all enhanced the game
and sometimes one would say
he kicks it back, from whence it came

From whence it came, from whence it came
kicks it back, from whence it came

You can still hear Peter Landy
"That's one goal each of two"
Peter Booth & Smokey, and our dear pal, Drew
Butch and Mike and Teddy, all the great old names
And sometimes one might say
he kicks it back, from whence it came

From whence it came, from whence it came
kicks it back, from whence it came

Jesaulenko, you beauty, just hit the boundary son
If ya don't mind umpire, the famous lines live on
We could be back here next week
the great moments in our game
And sometimes someone said
he kicks it back, from whence it came

From whence it came, from whence it came
Kicks it back, from whence it came

He Had His Gold Jacket On

WORDS: Greg Champion
TO THE TUNE OF: Always on my Mind

The gold jacket only comes out when Joffa is certain the Pies are gonna win. That's why it was exquisitely delicious when it was donned on Anzac Day 2009, with five minutes to go. The Pies led by fourteen points. With under a minute to go, the Bombers hit the front and held on. I have sung this ditty to Joffa at the Eltham Festival. He took it very well.

Only five minutes left now
in the big Anzac Day clash
Magpies leading by three goals
Bombers clearly done their dash
Zaharakis kicks a miracle
and over in the Pies cheer squad

He had his gold jacket on!
He had his gold jacket on!

You would think you'd be safe now
fourteen points up in time on
Bombers are not Houdinis
they looked well and truly gone
So he reaches into his bag
Thinking, cop this Essend-on

He put his gold jacket on!
He put his gold jacket on!

With less than one minute left to play
Zaharakis bangs away

He had his gold jacket on!
he had his gold jacket on!

From 2010

The West Sydney Suburb Of Penrith

WORDS: Greg Champion–Dave Priest
TO THE TUNE OF: El Paso

One of the most amusing ditties. It aims to capture all the culture and excitement of a Western Sydney Pokies club. An inspired thought from Dave of Mildura.

Out in the West Sydney suburb of Penrith
I fell in love with a Rooty Hill girl
There in the Leagues Club I shouted her middies
The pokies would ring, and their coloured lights whirl

Now Blacktown at night is not something to savour
lawless and dangerous, uncouth and crass
Liverpool, Bankstown, you wouldn't hang 'round there
but I was in love with my West Sydney lass

One night a Rugby League boofhead came in
Who'd just got out of the sin bi-i-in
Dashing and daring, a machine he was sharing
With saucy Sharlena, the sheila I loved – so, in anger I
Challenged this crim for the love of Sharlena
I shouted Rugby League's dead in this town!
Silence fell over the Rooty Hill bistro
Even the pokies they made not a sound

Just for a moment I stood there in horror
Shocked at my conduct, so reckless and dumb
Many thoughts raced through my mind as I stood there
I had but one chance and that was to run

Out through the kitchen, past all the trifles
Past all the veal parmagia-a-nas
Past all the spag bols, the donuts and jam rolls
I hid in the fridge til the danger was done – and so now, I
Find myself once again back in West Sydney
This time I can't hide my past and my fame
I'm here to coach football, not search for Sharlena
You see, the thing is, Kevin Sheedy's my name

Had A Gutful

WORDS: Greg Champion (no-one else would take the risk on this)
TO THE TUNE OF: Hawks Club song

From 2016, when the Hawks were at their 'least pleasant', on field. This ditty, perhaps understandably, drew a few retorts from displeased Hawks fans. Yes, I admit it's blunt.

Had a gutful of that Hawthorn
Don't they make you wanna spew
It would-n't be so bad if they played fair
But, everyone knows, they're mean and dirty
Number five and number fifteen
We know you know who you are
As for number three as well
That applies to you too
They are the mean and dirty Hawks

Hittin' The Snow

WORDS: Greg Champion (from an idea from Patti from Reservoir)
TO THE TUNE OF: King of the Road

This is straight up the guts DFS: Dees fans stereotyping.

Car chains for sale or rent
Conditions good to excellent
Snow gear the most recent
Goodbye football torment, ah but

Three hours in the Range Rover
Gets you up to Mt Buller, it's just
Five, to Hotham and we're
Hittin' the snow

I know every Helmut and every Heinz
Every different chalet's gluhwein
Every chairlift on every run
And someone said there's a footy game on, and

How nice to have three days to
Celebrate the Queen's birthday, and it's
Time to go, because we're
Hittin' the snow

They Kick It Sideways

WORDS: Greg Champion–Richard Evans
TO THE TUNE OF: My Way

A common fan lament in the modern game. Richard Evans has become *The Coodabeens'* most talented suggester of song ideas.

The game is in dispute
It's going right, down to the wire
The fans are off their heads
The tension couldn't get much higher
They win the ball down back
They need a score, they need it right away
So what, what do they do
They kick it siiiide-ways

Just moments to go, no ifs or buts
Only one way, straight up the guts
Turnover comes, just bomb it long
One minute more, the chance is gone
The game's about to slip away
They kick it siiiide-ways

Just moments to go, no ifs or buts
Only one way, straight up the guts
Turnover comes, just bomb it long
One minute more, the chance is gone
The game's about to slip away
They kick it siiiide-ways

From 2010

Welcome To What The ABC Calls Docklands

WORDS: Greg Champion–Anthony Thomas
TO THE TUNE OF: Hotel California

An epic tale to an epic tune. It was once alleged that it was very tricky to get into this ground.

Along Wurundjeri Highway, Footscray breeze in my hair
Stale smell of cigarette smoke, in the Docklands air
While approaching the concourse, I saw the stadium lights
Said welcome to Empty Head, good luck getting in tonight

In the queue at Gate five, I heard the quarter-time bell
I walked around and around just tryin' to find the right stairwell
I asked Customer Service, please show me the way
Just then a ground announcer boomed, on the big PA

Welcome to what ABC calls Docklands
It has other names, but they're sponsors' names
Plenty of room on level three at Docklands
Any time of year, no grass grows here

I'm not ASX-listed, I got no Mercedes Benz
I don't get into level two with, no corporate friends
Never been a member, of no Medallion club
My idea of well-connected is, mates down at the pub

I got no bartender bringing me my wine
I been sitting in the outer since 1959
I get a mid-strength beer, on a soggy tray
I couldn't care less what the interval announcer has to say

Last thing I remember as the lead see-sawed
Was popping out for a fag and trying to find the door
Stop, said the blue coat, where's your ticket please
You can get a passout but, you can never leave

Welcome to what ABC calls Docklands
It has other names, but they're sponsors' names
Plenty of room on level three at Docklands
Any time of year, no grass grows here

Incident In The Bullring

WORDS: Greg Champion–Peter Sim
TO THE TUNE OF: With a Swag upon my Shoulder

The goings-on in the Members, have long been a source of mirth to my *Coodabeens* colleagues. The fracas was real, evidently: the private schools tag-teaming, more imaginary.

With a patch upon both elbows
Tweed jackets and moleskins
We got into some fisticuffs
Last week in the bullring

Some said it was about the game
'Bout Magpies versus Dees
I heard something was said about
Scholarships at Haileybury

But there we were just chatting bout
The downturn in our shares
When six blokes walked into our bar
All dressed in Magpie gear

They clearly weren't our people
Didn't look like they would ski
They looked like those they won't let in
To the hotel at Portsea

Blair Paton-Smyth he copped a few
But gave as good as got
And those who went to Xavier
Helped those who went to Scotch!

A chap who went to Trinity
He also threw a few
And several from De La they showed
They could go a round or two

With a patch upon both elbows
Tweed jackets and moleskins
We got into some fisticuffs
Last week in the bullring

Give Heath A Chance

WORDS: John Ogge–Greg Champion
TO THE TUNE OF: Give peace a chance

John Ogge is among *The Coodabeens'* very top contributors: when he gets an idea, it's a goodie. He's the chap who dreamt up the hook *Members of the MCC* and conjured up this one too, about the former Collingwood defender, now the man down back at GWS.

Everybody's talkin' 'bout
Mick-ism, real-ism, what's the big deal-ism,
Blue-ism, truism, block-ism, buster-ism
Earth-ism, Ox-ism, what paradoxism

All we are saying, is give Heath a chance

Everybody's talkin' 'bout
Criticism, journalism, egotism, ostracism
Symbolism, paganism, cynicism, terrorism
Malthouse full house madhouse doghouse

All we are saying, is give Heath a chance

Everybody's talkin' 'bout
Lessons and teaching and learning and preaching
Scragging tagging bagging nagging
Bumping and jumping and ten goal thumpings
Cooney & Crossy, Mooney & Vossy, Roosy & Rossy

All we are saying, is give Heath a chance

Everybody's talkin' 'bout
tanking Beijing, clangers and hangers
Fixtures tricksters, grandstands and handstands
Roccas and Dockers and absolute shockers

All we are saying, is give Heath a chance

Everybody's talkin' 'bout
Osama Obama Jeff Farmer's karma
Buddy and Juddy, Gold Coast, goalposts
Contribution execution distribution substitution
Collingwood no good, chop them up for firewood

All we are saying, is give Heath a chance

It Is What It Is

WORDS: Greg Champion
TO THE TUNE OF: Let It Be

The Coodabeens are practised now in picking up the latest player/coach/media jargon.
   Coaches and players began leaning on this phrase quite heavily for a while, but thankfully it died off soon enough.

I watch the post match press conference
even though I shouldn't watch
'though I know it's bound to blow my mind

I hear the question arksed, and I
await the con-sidered reply
and the speaker doesn't let me down

It is what it is, it
is what it -- is, it is
what it is, it is what
is what it is

I wonder what it would be
if it wasn't what it clearly is
but, why wonder, it is, what it is

And though sometimes some things may not be
whatever they seem to be
you can trust me, it is what it is

It is what it is, it
is what it – is, it is
what it is, it is what
is what it is

Melbourne Is Closed

WORDS: Greg Champion–Noel Dennison
TO THE TUNE OF: King of the Road

People are understandably losing it as they try to commute in Melbourne these days.
   This was reinforced by the reaction to this, when sung on air. Clearly, people are struggling to cope.

Monash car park-freeway
Major works for twenty K
The charm of St Kilda Road
Forget it it's currently closed, and
If you try Hoddle Street
Pack your lunches for a week
And we – wish to warn the public
Melbourne is closed

The Ring Road round Keilor Way
It's a bunfight every day
Buses replacing trains
Cheer up, no pain no gain, and
As for the Tullamarine
A bigger mess you've never seen
And we – wish to warn the public
Melbourne is closed

Ya got level crossing works underway
Widening the Chandler Highway
And we – wish to warn the public
Melbourne is closed

Trav Kick A Goal

WORDS: Greg Champion–James Webster
TO THE TUNE OF: Gold

The Diamond Valley is notorious as a seething hotbed of Collingwoodism. Having lived there a fair while, I know this. Trying to pack as many North-Eastern suburbs as possible into one song was a fun job. This is a popular one with the other *Coodabeens*. I've had a roll at Bundoora tenpin bowl...

In their Craigieburn cars and the Broadmeadows bars
people are tuned to the trannie
Travis Cloke is lining up a shot
In the 'burbs, there are nervous grannies
queueing for fags at Campbellfield Coles
People out there, hoping Trav can kick a goal

In the tattoo parlours of Reservoir
people are tuned to the Maggies
In the shopping plazas of Epping and Lalor
people are bunched round the tellies
At Greensborough Bakery buying sausage rolls
People out there, hoping Trav can kick a goal

In the carparks of South Morang and Diamond Creek
the car radios are a-pumpin'
Travis has missed four shots in a row
and the Pies are coppin' a thumpin'
Over at Bundoora tenpin bowl
people out there, hoping Trav can kick a goal

Queueing for UDLs at Thomastown Coles
People out there, hoping Trav can kick a goal

Punt Road Oval

WORDS: Greg Champion–Stewart Handlebarz
TO THE TUNE OF: Bonny Banks of Loch Lomond

My favourite from the new album because I've adored the tune since my Dundonian father-in-law turned me onto it via a cassette by The Corries. The melody has all the power of Danny Boy, which is about as much power as exists in a song. A traditional Scottish song that can choke anyone up.

By yon bonny train lines, by yon Yarra Park
where the sun shines upon Punt Road Oval
There me and my cronies have sung the Tigers song
in the bonny parks around Punt Road Oval

So ye take the Swan Street, and I'll take the Bridge Road
and I'll be at Punt Road before ye
Where me and my cronies sing Tigerland again
in the bonny parks around Punt Road Oval

'Tis there that we worshipped, the feats of Royce Hart
Captain Blood, Jimmy Jess and old KB
'Tis there we've seen victories, and tragedies as well
singing hail Tigerland, Punt Road Oval

So ye take the Swan Street, and I'll take the Bridge Road
and I'll be at Punt Road before ye
Where me and my cronies sing Tigerland again
in the bonny parks around Punt Road Oval

The Hoodoo

WORDS: Greg Champion
TO THE TUNE OF: They Call the Wind Mariah

The hoodoo, aka Kennett's curse, extended to 11 games from Round 1, 2009, to the preliminary final of 2013. Not a bad run—from the Cats' viewpoint. GFF—good for footy!

In Western Vic they got a myth
it's bigger than the yeti
It's bigger than the meatball that
rolled off of the spaghetti

The hoodoo, the hoodoo
the Cats v Hawthorn hoodoo

In olden times in Glenferrie
a cowboy from the bayou
apparently insulted the
genteel folk of Corio

The hoodoo, the hoodoo
the Cats v Hawthorn hoodoo

And legend says, that since that time
relations have been wartorn
It seems a curse was placed upon
extended, greater Hawthorn

And no-one knows how long it takes
to undo such a hoodoo
They only know, each time they play
the Hawks end up in do-do

The hoodoo, the hoodoo
the Cats v Hawthorn hoodoo

From 2010

This Stand Is Our Stand

WORDS: Greg Champion–Richard Evans
TO THE TUNE OF: This Land is Our Land

Members stereotyping. Again, we're lucky that the Members find it more amusing than most others.

As I was walking to the Members' entrance
I saw some public, but I kept my distance
It baffles me how they get guest passes
When this stand was made for folk like me

This stand is our stand, it isn't your stand
It isn't there for those unwashed Pies fans
This stand has cloakrooms and proper lounges
This stand was made for folk like me

Before the game I attend a luncheon
I don't eat fast food, prefer a function
I went to a top school I observe dress standards
This stand is there for folk like me

This ground is our ground, this ground's not your ground
We had it first and it's always been ours
From the Members' Long Room to the new Museum
This ground belongs to us not you

This ground is our ground, this ground's not your ground
You can come and play here, but do not hang around
Please stay at Swan Street at the Swimming Centre
This ground belongs to us not you

Everybody Hates The Hawks

WORDS: Greg Champion
TO THE TUNE OF: Rainy day women

After decades of relentless baiting of the Maggies and their fans by *The Coodabeens*, the Linda Crescent/Waverley mob has seized the chalice as the least likeable club; and it doesn't sit well with some Hawks-loving *Coodabeens* listeners. Seventy is the new sixty. Fifty is the new forty. Hawthorn is the new Collingwood.

Well certain things in footy never change
What is more, they tend to stay the same
Like Heath Shaw is always giving lip
Like the Dees can't win a Premiership
Like Bruce Doull was never known to talk
And – everybody hates the Hawks

Now for decades KB took a stand
And wouldn't go back to Tigerland
Some say Dees fans are always up the snow
But whether that is true I would not know
But as sure as cheese isn't chalk
Everybody hates the Hawks

Now Pies fans, get lotsa mockery
But they've always given back what they receive
The Tigers so often finish ninth
We can only hope they will this time
But the biggest truth of all in the sport
Is everybody hates the Hawks

Yes as sure as pigs produce pork
Everybody hates the Hawks

Oh St Kilda

WORDS: Greg Champion–Martin Harris
TO THE TUNE OF: Hallelujah

Footy's most under-achieving side? You gotta feel for Saints fans.

A haunted team since '66
since Barry Breen's immortal kick
They say what doesn't kill ya almost kills ya
They remind, at different times
of fantasies and nursery rhymes
Of Goldilocks, Pooh Bear and Bob the Builder

Oh St Kilda, oh St Kilda
Oh St Kilda

We've had all kinds of knuckleheads
Ones with helmets ones with dreads
that looked like Genghis Khan and Tutankhamun
In '97 glory beckoned
Stan Alves had us there we reckoned
But who the hell was standing Darren Jarman?

Oh St Kilda, oh St Kilda
Oh St Kilda

Things looked good when Malcolm Blight
rode in as a shining knight
But that collapsed and left us all bewildered
Even now with top draft picks
Yet somehow the outlook's sick
And doubt disgust despair confusion fill ya

Oh St Kilda, oh St Kilda
Oh St Kilda

By The Time We Get To Yarck

WORDS: Greg Champion–Richard Evans
TO THE TUNE OF: By the time I get to Phoenix

Snow-themed Dees songs have become their own sub group. For fear of annoying the odd Dees fan, the vast majority are not included—but some, like this one, are included as they are more...gentle.

By the time we've cleared the snow and, got those chains off
The Demons will have run onto the ground
And as we take our tea and scones in Mansfield
it's odds on they'll be three or four goals down

By the time we get to Yarck, kids will be yawning
We'll stop at that cafe-art gallery
We'll buy a small Hans Heysen for the guestroom
As the radio says Dees are on their knees

By the time we hit the ring road, kids are sleepin'
We'll roll through Ivanhoe and on to Kew
And the Old Boys will be texting from the Bullring
And Hamish says we wish we'd come with you

And he says next year, we're coming too

Bernie Vince Used Cars

WORDS: Greg Champion–Richard Evans
TO THE TUNE OF: Cool for cats

Bernie Vince is a *Coodabeens* favourite. I once played a birthday gig at the Stansbury Hall, Yorke Peninsula, SA. I asked a twelve-year-old boy from the audience to join me on stage to sing *Red Hot Go*. The locals assured me that that twelve-year-old would one day play for the Crows. That kid was Bernie Vince!

If you're in South Australia and you need a car that's new
on Lower North East Road's the bloke who'll do it right for you
Now here's a little Datsun that a Klemzig granny owned
and drove to church on Sundays till they put her in a home
There's sawdust in the gearbox but the wheel rims have been chromed
a spin around the block and you are sure to be convinced
Another happy customer –
in another used car sold by Bernie Vince – Bernie Vince

Meanwhile out at West Lakes on the other side of town
The Crowboys and the Ferals play the twenty-sixth Showdown
The Ferals are on top, the Crows are running out of steam
they need someone to stand up and do something for the team
And whammo, here's the pretty boy, the number seventeen
He dobs to Taylor Walker as across the ground he sprints
Another happy customer –
getting top delivery from Bernie Vince – Bernie Vince

Sorry I Made You Follow Melbourne

WORDS: Peter Bellairs–Greg Champion
TO THE TUNE OF: Sorry

Peter Bellairs is the dad of our Coodabeen member/producer Andy Bellairs. This is one of the least re-written ideas we've received. Peter explained it as: by way of an apology to my sons. He included an explanation of Melruckles—evidently, a small soft toy Demons doll. The family are not skiers, but he went along with the myth.

It's cold down at the Darklands
The Dees go down again
My boys ain't seen the Demons win
Since I don't know when

I'm sorry that I made you follow Melbourne
I'm sorry for the pain and misery
More than anything else I'm sorry for my health
So let's just go and ski

Your friends all follow Hawthorn
They win every game
All you can do is pack your skis
And not complain

Roosy says they're trying
They're trying me for sure
Roosy says they're dying
To kick a winning score

I'm sorry that I gave you both Melruckles
Sorry "The Grand Old Flag" has been no use
But forget everyone else, I'm most sorry for myself
And I hope it's not child abuse?

I'm sorry that I made you follow Melbourne
I'm sorry for the pain and misery
More than anything else I'm sorry for my health
So let's just go and ski

Viva North Melbourne

WORDS: Greg Champion
TO THE TUNE OF: Viva Las Vegas

A lady emailed *The Coodabeens* in 2017 and protested that we never sing songs about North Melbourne, on *The Coodabeens'* show. So here we are trying to right that wrong.

The bright lights and big sights of Curzon street
gonna set your soul on fire
Don't waste your money on that Docklands wheel
North Melbourne's got all you desire
Get a top take-away on Victoria Street
The darts at the Albion are hard to beat
The Errol street butcher sells quality meat
Viva North Melbourne! Viva North Melbourne!

Oh how I wish I was down on Arden Street
With so many pokies to play
And Queensberry and Chetwynd Streets keep pumpin'
twenty-four hours in the day
Every night is something different, oh yeah
all the thrills and spills of the fair
I don't even know if the gasometer's still there
Viva North Melbourne! Viva North Melbourne!

Get a top takeaway on Victoria Street
The darts at the Albion are hard to beat
The Errol street butcher sells quality meat
Viva North Melbourne! Viva North Melbourne!
Viva, viva, North Melbourne!

Another Truck Got Stuck Underneath The Montague Street Bridge

WORDS: Greg Champion–Greg Tuck
TO THE TUNE OF: Ode to Billy Joe

Whatever big news is *breaking*, all over the world—and it's no news unless it's *breaking*—you can rely on another truck getting stuck under that dreaded bridge in South Melbourne.

---

it was a big news week
Down in Europe lots was goin' on
The Poms had a vote to quit the EU
Suddenly they're gone
But that was nothing compared to
The outcome of a soccer game
When a tiny little North Pole country
Shot to sudden world fame
And just when you thought
There could be no more world carnage
Another truck got stuck
Underneath the Montague Street Bridge

As if there hadn't, in the world this week
Already been enough dam-age
Another truck got stuck
Underneath the Montague Street Bridge

A more devastating news flash
It's difficult to envis-age
Another truck getting stuck
Underneath the Montague Street Bridge

Fat Side Of The Ground

WORDS: Greg Champion–Peter Sim
TO THE TUNE OF: Always Look on the Bright Side of Life

Of all the terms in modern football jargon, the fat side holds a certain exalted place.
How did it come about? I had to ask my colleagues what it meant. You also want to ask—why??
A top thought from our stalwart Pete.

Sometimes you get the ball
You don't know what to do
You wish you had a friend standing near
Just do not wear a frown
Just take a look around
And the answer soon becomes, crystal clear

Always kick to the fat side of the ground
Way out wide where no-one's ever around

Don't go up the guts
Up the guts is nuts
That's what all the dumb players do
Kick it round the sides
Take it really wide
You know you should do it, shouldn't you

Always kick to the fat side of the ground
Way out wide where no-one's ever around

If you see the game congest
Then round the back is best
Even if it's ugly and it's sad
Don't be apologetic
It might look unaesthetic
But bomb it to the fat side, you'll be glad

Always kick to the fat side of the ground
Way out wide where no-one's ever around

We Hate Youse

WORDS: John Ogge–Greg Champion
TO THE TUNE OF: Silly love songs

I flippantly admit that Pies bashing songs have almost paid off my house.
  At other times I attest that Pies baiting is a testament to the power and might of Magpie fanaticism—a kind of backhanded compliment. Some buy that—some don't...

You'd think that people would have had enough of hate-the-Pies songs
I read the emails and I see it isn't so
And what's wrong with that, I'd like to know, so here we go, again

We hate youse, yes we do
We hate youse, we really do

You'd think that over time the *Coodabeens* might do some anti-Hawks songs
Or for a change that we might give it to the Blues
Well, we do sometimes, but then we go, back to Pies, again

We hate youse, yes we do
We hate youse, we truly do

Travis To The Twos

WORDS: Greg Champion–Andrew Ryan
TO THE TUNE OF: Tangled up in blue

A bit like Fev, Trav was never far from the headlines.

Down on Swan Street, Monday morning
Nathan meets with Ed
Something big has gotta give
they're calling for our heads
They look straight at each other
sensing their mortality
Tough decisions must be made
as they sip on cups of tea
Nathan knows the time has come
that Trav must pay his dues
Something desperate must be done
Lord knows he's had issues kicking true –
Travis to the twos

In the 'burbs at Montmorency
fans at breaking point
if the Maggies don't win soon
they're gonna trash the joint
Daisy, Harry, Heath Shaw gone
Swanny's been laid low
Marley Williams, Jamie Elliott
how low can this go
Goldsack, Reid and Langdon too
adding to their pain
And even now Jesse White's
still not getting a game
Plus, you know who
Travis to the twos

Meanwhile in the VFL
Travis clunks a mark
Slot this from the square and it
could re-ignite the spark
But it don't go through
Travis to the Blues

Streets Of Hotham

WORDS: Greg Champion–John Ogge
TO THE TUNE OF: Streets of London

From 2018. Ah, cultural stereotyping, a term I learnt from *The Coodabeens*, marches on in ditties like this.

Have you seen the manager of the almost empty chalet
staring at the bookings site, which tells a tale of woe
Above his head a TV where the Dees are up by ninety points
Seems nobody wants to book a chalet in the snow

So what will become of all the ski resorts
and of our whole snow industry
Let me take you by the hand and lead you through the streets of Hotham
I'll show you a ghost town, thanks to the good ole Dees

Have you seen the face of the chair lift operator
Fanny's Run's a shadow of its halcyon days
You can get three rides, for the usual price of one today
but nobody's riding, 'cos they've all stayed away

Have you seen the Toorak tractor-driving retired Brighton couple
who do not follow football, perched forlornly at the bar
Briefly sharing comments with a passing Heinz and Helmut
they shake their heads and wonder where all the people are

So what will become of all the ski resorts
and of our whole snow industry
Let me take you by the hand and lead you through the streets of Hotham
I'll show you a ghost town, thanks to the good ole Dees

There Is A Very Special State

WORDS: Greg Champion
TO THE TUNE OF: House of the Rising Sun

The question that won't go away: should Tassie have a side?

There is a very special state
They call Tasmania
And they're way down there, down south somewhere
Off the bottom of Australia

The people there are quite similar
To folks like me and you
They love their footy and now they're saying
We want a team in too

They say don't overlook us
Don't write us off too soon
This is the state that's given you
A talking doll of David Boon

We've got some okay stadia
We know we can pull a crowd
And we promise that we'll try and make
Our sirens sound real loud

And if we get a team down here
We guarantee we will
Not go putting matches on
Anywhere near pulp mills

What other state has got a bigger
Chocolate factory
No other state has brought the world
Fresh King Island brie

Now Hobart's population
Is smaller than Geelong's
And the island's population is
Two and a half Wollongongs

It's a lovely place to visit
And it's a lovely place to stay
But will they get their football team
You'll have to ask Andre

Wycheproof Linesman

WORDS: Greg Champion–Michael Paterson
TO THE TUNE OF: Wichita Lineman

One of the most enjoyed and requested ditties. If I recall rightly, Michael Paterson emailed and just suggested the name switch. And Wyche is such a ripper place, a classic Victorian bush town. Way beyond Wyche is Berriwillock, and I once sang there on the reserve by the pub.

I am a line marker at Wyche
have been for a long time
and every Saturday I'm out there early
marking the lines
I mix the paint up in the doo-dad
it relaxes my mind
and the Wycheproof linesman
is out marking lines

My job is Telecom technician
nine to five on weekdays
Although the Telco keeps on sacking us or
chopping our pay
I run the phone lines to a farm house
I do internet these days
And the Wycheproof linesman
still does it his way

I do the tennis courts in summer
help out on the weekends
I bag the courts and water them
before games, and after again
I officiate in matches
any job, I don't mind
And the Wycheproof linesman
loves working the lines

I used to be a VicRoads worker
holding lollypop signs
But the job that I liked best was on the highways
marking the lines
I'd do the one down the middle
I liked the ones on the sides
And the Wycheproof linesman
Is still working the lines

Where Will You Go To Sir Jimmy

WORDS: Greg Champion–Noel Dennison
TO THE TUNE OF: Where do you go to my lovely

As the Great Essendon Saga was still unrolling itself in 2014, Sir James understandably sought refuge *au continent*.

They say the South, c'est si bon
with the lavender fields of Provence
Rent a cottage in a chic little village
many miles from mad Moonee Ponds

Or the charms of the Burgundy region
with the fortified towns near Dijon
Where the wineries and the cathedrals
will appeal to the best bon vivants

So where will you go to Sir Jimmy
avec la femme and enfants
Les Alpes and Bretagne await you
what a magnifique vaca-tion

Or why not straight to St Mauritz
and hobnob it with the jet set
A casino in Monte Carlo
and squeeze in a round of roulette

You can keep one eye on le website
to see how Les Bombers may fare
While you soak up the sights in The Pyrenees
and pop into Spain while you're there

And take la famille to gay Paris
to Le Louvre, Le Tour, Le Sorbonne
Montmartre will remind you of Strathmore
and grab a snap at L'Arc De Triomphe

So where will you go to Sir Jimmy
avec la femme and enfants
La joie de vivre does await you
what a magnifique vaca-tion

Through The Windscreens Of Their Cars

WORDS: Greg Champion–Greg Tuck
TO THE TUNE OF: Windmills of your mind

Across more than thirty-odd years we *Coodabeens* have had the great pleasure of travelling to countless country football clubs to entertain. We once got a map out and started pinpointing them all. We have sampled the kiosk soup and admired the ladies who made it, smelt the barbie, heard the smack of damp boot on damp leather, negotiated with the ticket clicker on the gate, and spoken with those who mark the lines at eight in the morning.

Round the oval they are gathered
Nearly every car in town
And they toot their horns together
as the players take the ground
It has rained throughout the morning
and it won't be stopping soon
as they nestle in their cars
settled for the afternoon

And the girls are playing netball
and around the courts it's packed
And when the games are over
to the oval they flock back
just to cheer the local stars
through the windscreens of their cars

With their thermoses of soup
with their ginger wine and port
and the kiosk trade is roaring
as more pies and chips are bought
And they go back to their cars
and they scoff on sausage rolls
and soon the horns are blaring
because someone's kicked a goal

And the girls are playing netball
and around the courts it's packed
And when the games are over
to the oval they flock back
just to cheer the local stars
through the windscreens of their cars

A Good Game Of Footy

Greg Champion [BMG Publishing]

L.I.T.P.—living in the past. One of many 'protest' songs about modern stats, jargon and coverage.

The term, 'A Good Game Of Footy' was noted by the brainy Richard Evans as a good song idea; by chance, the same phrase was already on my list. Trash Treseder also contributed here.

I don't wanna hear 'bout – intercepts
hear 'bout – pressures acts
hear 'bout – goal assists, and
I don't wanna hear 'bout – score involvements
hear 'bout – rebound 50s
hear 'bout – clearance efficiency

I just want a good – game of footy
good – game of footy, good – game of footy
I just want a good – game of footy
And I don't care 'bout all that other stuff

I don't wanna hear 'bout – metres gained
hear 'bout – contested ball
hear 'bout – fantasy points, and
I don't care about – lowering eyes
care about – fat sides and clangers
care about – last ten scoring shots, and

I just want a good – game of footy
good – game of footy, good – game of footy
I just want a good – game of footy
And I don't care 'bout all that other stuff

I don't want a replay – of a free kick
from a – different angle
while the – game continues, and
I don't want a camera – on the boundary
or be – hind the goals, just on the
wing, and leave it there, and

I just want a good – game of footy
good – game of footy, good – game of footy
I just want a good – game of footy
And I don't care 'bout all that other stuff

Hello Doggies

WORDS: Greg Champion–Leigh Kibby
TO THE TUNE OF: Hello Dolly

With the demise of Fitzroy, Footscray, aka Western Bulldogs, might have become everybody's second side. The 2016 charge to the flag is already folklore. They'd waited so long. A fairytale.

Hello Doggies, yes hello Doggies
it's so good to see you here at finals time
You're playing beaut Doggies, rooty-toot Doggies
You been growin', you keep showin' how you're goin' strong

I hear your song Doggies, sing along Doggies
yes, that old familiar song Sons of the 'Scray, so
Structure up Doggies, dream about that Cup Doggies
Doggies go out and win that flag today

I hear your song Doggies, sing along, Doggies
Yes, that old familiar song, Sons of the 'Scray, so
Structure up Doggies, dream about that Cup Doggies
Doggies go out and win that flag today

Protected Zone

Greg Champion [BMG publishing]

From 2018. Since this was done the howls of horror with this rule have reached fever pitch. This thought came while watching footy—most do—and I didn't bother seeking an existing tune. It became its own thing.

I'm lyin' in bed
I'm havin' a nightmare
I've wandered into
the protected zone

Protected zone
Protected zone
Lord don't let me walk into
the protected zone

There's people burning
They're burning in fire
And on a big throne
Sits the devil umpire

Protected zone
Protected zone
Lord don't let me walk into
The protected zone

Beware of this warning
It could happen to you
If you should wander
Wander into, the

Protected zone
Protected zone
I'm havin' a nightmare 'bout
The protected zone

Where Have All The Roberts Gone

WORDS: Greg Champion (From an idea from Richard Evans)

This is pure L.I.P.: living in the past.

Where have all the Roberts gone
Walls and Flower
Diperdomenico
Groenewegen
Where have all the Barries gone
Cable Davis Robran Round
Young names now everyone's
Jaydens Braydens Kaydens

Where have all the Garys gone
Dempsey Wilson
Where have all the Kevins gone
Murray Sheedy
Where have all the Dermotts gone
Ha ha, there was only one
Young names now everyone's
Jaydens Braydens Kaydens

Where have all the Bobbies gone
Skilton Davis
Where have all the Jimmys gone
Krakouer Buckley
Where have all the Peters gone
Daicos Bedford Hudson Knights
Young names now everyone's
Jaydens Braydens Kaydens

Where have all the long bombs gone
To Royce and Huddo
Where have proper jumpers gone
Hoops sashes stripes
Where have proper jumpers gone
Giant birdheads everyone
Teal purple indigo
I blame Demetriou

Your Team's No Good

WORDS: Greg Champion–David Blom
TO THE TUNE OF: Seasons of Change

This one evokes fond memories for *The Coodabeens*, and hopefully our listeners, because it is so evocative of our youth, and of 'prog rock'.

See the sun shining on the ground
Bright dressed folk, throng around
See them throw themselves at a ball
Sportsmen all, short and tall

Strange folk waving their arms around
So many sights and sounds
Drinks and fine fare that taste so nice
If you can pay the price

The season goes so quickly
Though now it's just begun
From April 'til September
Until there's only one
Mine's better than your team
Your team's no good!

In the towers the lords they plan
Where to place every man
Wild men running while people call
Chasing all, one red ball

Strange folk waving their arms around
So many sights and sounds
Drinks and fine fare that taste so nice
If you can pay the price

The season goes so quickly
Though now it's just begun
From April 'til September
Until there's only one
Mine's better than your team
Your team's no good!

Oh Jimmy Stynes

WORDS: Greg Champion
TO THE TUNE OF: Danny Boy

Upon the loss of Jimmy Stynes, in March 2012.

Oh Jimmy boy, the pipes, the pipes have called you
From glen to glen, and down the mountain side
The summer's gone, and all the leaves have fallen
'Tis you, 'tis you must go and we must bide

But come ye back when summer's in the meadow
Or when the valley's hushed and white with snow
And to the 'G with you to see the Dees we'll go
Oh Jimmy boy, oh Jimmy boy, we love you so

From 2010

The Fundamentals

Greg Champion [BMG publishing]

To be spoken, over a slow country instrumental, such as old dogs and children and watermelon wine. The poem arose from a 2018 discussion on *The Coodabeens* probing a key question: what *are* the fundamentals of the game.

Well I came home from work, I said hi, son
And my little boy had the radio on
They were chatting away on the Coodabeens
And my little boy asked me... what does fundamentals mean?

So I sat my boy down, I said if you really wanna know
For you son, you know I'll give it a go
But before I give the fundamentals a good shot
First I'd better tell you... just what they're not

Son, when you see players raise their hands before they ruck
And when you see grey jumpers, that make you wanna chuck
And fat sides, dribble kicks and metres gained
And deafening announcements during the game

I said as sure as the night sky is filled with pretty stars
That's NOT what fundamentals are

I said, it's big men who never get any smaller
And little guys who never get any taller
I said it's A-B-C-D on the scoreboard
and coaches with the full support of the board

I said, it's playing in black boots, and playing man on man
It's reserves in dressing gowns, and beer in cans
I said long bombs to Royce is a fundamental thing
but the biggest one of all...is a camera...on the wing

And my little boy hugged me, and he said 'thanks Dad'
He said I guess the fundamentals aren't all that bad
And tonight when he's tucked in, in his little cosy bed
there'll be visions of fundamentals...running around in his head

THE
OTHERS

Gigs have been the bread and butter of my past 45 years. And 90 per cent of those gigs have involved performing footy songs. So, when you can escape those songs, such as at festivals like Port Fairy (although not entirely!), it makes for a lovely change. Because, conversely, 90 per cent of the songs I write are *not* about football. So here are some non-footy offerings.

And yes, a key non-footy topic herein, is the suburbs of Melbourne. Where did this obsession with Melbourne suburbs spring from? I don't know. I have two theories: suburb references amuse *The Coodabeens*—maybe for the same reason that stand-up comedian Simon Thorpe used to recite, live at gigs, all the stations on any Melbourne train line. It amuses. The other factor may be that I set out when young to try to write Aussie themes into songs at a time when overseas place names, mainly USA ones, dominated. It helps fulfil a desire to draw on local themes.

When I was 17 I wrote down a quote I came across: *Publishing a volume of poetry is like dropping a rose petal down the Grand Canyon and waiting for an echo.* Many of us write poetry at times—against our better judgment! Some of us more than others. And we haven't even got close yet to waiting for that echo. Sometimes a poem just spews out and you can't prevent its birth. A poem may only be useful if it can touch someone else. I hope something here can touch someone.

Melbourne Town

Greg Champion [BMG Publishing]

A late-night cruise around the Melbourne pub gigs of the early eighties.

If you look down on Barkly Street
you might see them on the beat
Luna Park, The Esplanade
good enough for a postcard
Acland Street I knew her well
Bananas and The Village Belle
We'll do the crawl down Chapel Street
cruisin' for a midnight eat

We're just out doin' the rounds
toolin' around in Melbourne Town

Carlisle Street for laundromats
Fitzroy Street for Space Invaders
the old rambling share house
drop-in spot for freaks and sages
Cleopatra's for falafels
Leo's if you're dining late
I bought a Guild Starfire down that street
wish I still had her today

We're just out doin' the rounds
Toolin' around in Melbourne Town

Warrigal road someone said
is officially where the world would end
Any further East than that
you are off the edge my friend
The Cosmo and The Prince Of Wales
the Espy with its seedy scene
Occasionally to venture out
to beer barns like the Village Green

We're just out doin' the rounds
Toolin' around in Melbourne Town

I'll take you 'cross the river to
those Brunswick and those Carlton parts
Come with me we're gonna see
Andrew Pendlebury playin' at Hearts
Through Collingwood and Richmond to
the Tiger Lounge we'll ride tonight
But never did I live this way
Always stayed St Kilda side

We're just out doin' the rounds
Toolin' around in Melbourne Town

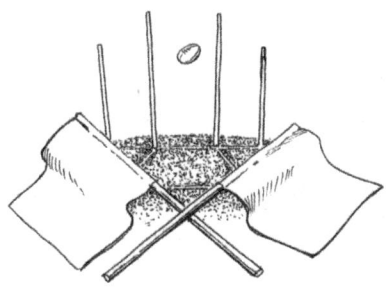

On Every Hand There Is A Finger

WORDS: Greg Champion
TO THE TUNE OF: Turn turn turn

From 1990. What can I say.

On every hand
there is a finger
and at the end of every finger
there is a fingernail

In every kitchen
there is a freezer
and inside of every freezer
there are fish fingers

So let us stand up
and let us sit down
let us jump up
and fall on the ground
Let us take things
and smash them all up
Then let us put those smashed things back together

In every schoolbag
there is a lunchbox
and inside every lunchbox
there is a sandwich

So take time to groan
and take time to grunt
take time to wear your
shirt back to front
to go to the races
and have a good punt
a time when you must walk away from punting

For every song
there is a singer
and for everything that's brought
there is a bringer

Organ Donation Song

WORDS: Greg Champion
TO THE TUNE OF: Achy Breaky Heart

This cheeky piece eventually got me an invitation to sing it at Parliament House at our nation's capital, in an Organ Donation event.

You can have my heart
and other body parts
I'm not gonna need 'em when I go
You can have my hands
my tonsils or my glands
Just help yourself
I won't even know

You can have my guts
my kidneys or my butt
Be my guest, no-one's keeping score
Have my belly button
to me it don't mean nuttin'
Just chop it out and scrape it off the floor

You can have my head
as soon as I am dead
Though no-one needs a pre-loved head these days
Let my body work
for medical research
I'm only going to slowly rot away

You can have my nose
everything must go
Just take it all, no-one's keeping tabs
Take my cornea
I'll have no idea
But certain parts, they're not up for grabs

Just don't take my thing
my little ding-a-ling
I just don't think he'd understand
He belongs to me
and I don't wanna see
him doing work for any other man

I Still Call South Australia Home

WORDS: Greg Champion
TO THE TUNE OF: I Still Call Australia Home

Well, it's my state of origin. She calls me, and I yearn to return to her.

I've seen the harbour lights of tinsel town
I've seen the Yarra, it's nice, but it's brown
I have wandered from Woodenbong to Bendigo
But I still call South Australia home

I'm always travellin' I love being free
From Noosa to Surfers to Mullumbimby
But no matter how interesting Australia can be
I still call South Australia home

All the lovely wineries
Their passion for footy
Their disdain for Victorians
You can take the one tram
From town to Glenelg, and
You can ride it back to town again

One day I'll shop again in Rundle Mall
I'll go see the Crows play some brilliant *foopball*
I'll admire Tea Tree Plaza and how much it's grown
And I still call South Australia home

I Am An Old Wingman

WORDS: Greg Champion–John Kraszlan
TO THE TUNE OF: Angel of Montgomery

Our noble game of footy can sometimes drift into the sphere of art.
That great 'No Man's Land' in between footy and art—is where we explore.

I am an old battler
Famed for my smother
My old number's another
Memory that's been sold
Our kicks were thumpers
Our handballs inspired
But that was the Sixties
And so long ago

Show me a wingman
that flew for old Fitzroy
Make me a rover, for
one more cameo
Just give me a loose ball
that I can run on to
Playing for the jumper
was the one way to go

When I was a young lad
I kicked in the backyard
I kicked with the neighbours
in Port Melbourne streets
Now I just turn up
to the reunions
relive the memories
the fading old dreams

Show me a wingman
that flew for old Fitzroy
Make me a rover, for
one more cameo
Just give me a loose ball
That I can run on to
Playing for the jumper
was the one way to go

The French Song

WORDS: Divishti Rankine–Greg Champion
TO THE TUNE OF: La Vie En Rose

This is perhaps the most requested of all non-footy ditties, since about 1991 when I heard Judy Small sing it at Port Fairy Festival. I asked her about it and she said she learnt it from Divishti Rankine. I then added the second half. The song has led to appearances on *Hey Hey It's Saturday*, a Comedy Festival Gala and a French Embassy Bastille day brekky. And—in France—at a Country Music festival near Rouen, and at the Australian Embassy in Paris. Many years later I met Divishti again; *merci*.

Pâté escargots soup de jour
cordon bleu chic coiffure
fait accompli maison
crème de menthe Marcel Marceau
meringue blancmange Bardot
gauche gay Paris garcon
gendarme agent provocateur
eau de toilette voyeur
au revoir déjà vu
carte blanche bidet croissant bourgeois
c'est la vie abattoir
bon voyage coup d'état
hors d'ouevres Peugeot faux pas
Gerard Dépardieu

Lacoste panache papier mâché
en suite rue morgue Yoplait
Pepe La Pew soufflé
en tous cas le Guy Forget
Maurice Chevalier le Rainbow Warrior
lingerie chocolat éclair
avant garde Frigidaire
fromage crouton Cointreau
cherchez la femme boudoir je t'aime
vol au vent Jacques Cousteau
joie de vive Plastic Bertrand
le Coq Sportif penchant
Henri Leconte

I Am A Fitzroy Fugitive

Greg Champion [BMG Publishing]

From 2013. We were shooting a band clip on the steps of Fitzroy Town Hall when this notion bubbled up.

I am a Fitzroy fugitive
From Carlton have I come
Originally from Collingwood
I live on the run
I don't go 'cross Hoddle
That's too far for me
I'll die in Fitzroy yes
And happy I'll be

I was born in Abbotsford
Way back in '21
The son of a drifter
From Richmond he'd come
And if I should be born again
Can I make it clear
I really would hope
That it happens right here

I've heard tell of Preston
They say it's no good
They say that it's almost
Like Collingwood
I met someone once
Said to Northcote they'd been
But I'll die in Fitzroy
And I'll die happily

'Tween Brunswick and Wellington
I've roamed back and forth
Though I never did want to
Go to Fitzroy North
A true Fitzroy fugitive
I always will be
And I hope that I die
'Fore they catch up with me

Try the Napier Hotel
If you're looking for me

Geelong, Geelong

WORDS: Greg Champion
TO THE TUNE OF: New York, New York

Geelong: the New York of central-west Victoria. Boasting The Sphinx, the (much-mourned) waterslide, the (extinct) Ocean Child Hotel, the late night potato cake shop at the bottom of La Trobe Terrace for those hungry trips home. Its charms abound.

Start spreadin' the news
I'm catchin' the train
I'm gonna take that V-line to
Geelong, Geelong

I'm going to ride that Ferris wheel
at Eastern Beach
and grab some new tracky dacks
from Dimmeys at Little Malop Street

Those sights of Geelong
you just gotta see 'em
you will be knocked out by the
National Wool Museum

And we'll admire those fine You Yangs
on our way through
We'll visit Werribee Mansion – and –
Werribee Zoo, too!

That Lord of the Isles
it's calling my name
I'm going to have a pot and toast
Geelong, Geelong

Then we'll have several pots
in Cameron Ling's nightspots
Corio calls, Geelong, Geelong!

God Bless The Developer

Greg Champion [BMG publishing]

I lived on a windy dirt road and an undesirable development brought big trucks down this road, pulling down overhead cables. Fred Dagg deliciously declared that the role of the Real Estate agent is to add money to something without actually doing anything to it.

Beloved ones, let us all give praise
To those professions that brighten our days
Let us single out one that lightens our way
God bless the developer

The developer turns something into something more
Put something there that wasn't there before
Makes something new from something tired and old
Turns a carpark into a pot of gold, so

Let us give thanks to the people out there
Who demonstrate a genuine care
Those who contribute more than their fair share
God bless the developer

The developer can take a simple stretch of sand
Build a hotel, opulent and grand
Make a shopping centre from a boring block of land
Oh, yes they can

Build a skyscraper with a whole pile of dough
Get someone to buy it and watch your money grow
Build apartment complexes of every size and sort
Plough the profit into a time share resort, so

Dearly beloved let us all feel blessed
By those who serve society the best
Those who exhibit sincere selflessness
God bless the developer

Just Don't Mention Tibet

WORDS: Baden Smith–Greg Champion
TO THE TUNE OF: Jailhouse rock

The plight of Tibet is a cause very close to me. Due to this ditty I will now be on a secret service blacklist.

Went to the Olympics in old Beijing
I was selected in the weightlifting
Team officials said go for gold
but before we left everybody got told
They said – team management said
this is an order, and don't forget:
just don't mention Tibet

Yeah – just don't mention Tibet
just don't mention Tibet
You're only gonna get 'em upset
just don't mention Tibet
You can drink and smoke cigarettes
just don't mention Tibet

Now the Taiwan issue is a no-go zone
if you say Falun Gong you're on the plane home
Don't even think about Tiananmen Square
And The Dalai Lama, just don't go there
They said – team management said
You can drink and smoke cigarettes
just don't mention Tibet

Yeah – just don't mention Tibet
Just don't mention Tibet
you're only gonna get 'em upset
Just don't mention Tibet
You can drink and smoke cigarettes
just don't mention Tibet

Keepin' The Dream Alive

Greg Champion [BMG Publishing]

Some of the other *Coodabeens* are more up with the machinations of the media than me. I learnt from them that *Keepin' The Dream Alive* was the slogan of a certain golden-tonsilled legend Sydney broadcaster: the one who dominated commercial radio, put out poetry books and Country music compilations, pushed the merits of Valvoline…and kept his dream alive for so long.

I'm just a broadcaster doin' my job
Oh yeah, uh-huh
I'm an honest battler who's in touch with the mob
Oh yeah, uh-huh
I'm a down-to-earth bloke whose record is clean
And so is my car, thanks to Valvoline
And let me tell you all about my four-wheel drive
While I'm keepin' the dream alive, oh yeah
Keepin' the dream alive

I'm an average Aussie tryin' to make a buck
And I'm keepin' the dream alive
If I find a stray million that's just good luck
And I'm keepin' the dream alive
I don't wanna talk about sponsors' cheques
I do wanna talk about Castrol GTX
I'm just doin' my bit 'til the limo arrives
And I'm keepin' the dream alive, oh yeah
Keepin' the dream alive

I'm not looking for fame or glory
Just I'm keepin' the dream alive
I just wanna tell the other side of the story
And I'm keepin' the dream alive
Some people just wanna bag the banks
I believe they deserve our heartfelt thanks
Hey, I'm just like you, just tryin' to survive
And let me tell you all about my four-wheel drive
While I'm keepin' the dream alive, uh-huh
Keepin' the dream alive

The Wild Colonial PM

WORDS: Greg Champion–Jane Harris
TO THE TUNE OF: Wild Colonial Boy

At one point during Kevin Rudd's tenure at the top he drew plenty of scorn for uttering the term *fair shake of the sauce bottle*.

There was a bonza battler bloke
and Kevin was his name
He said at talkin' Strine me chums
I'm a natural at the game
He said fair dinkum ridgy didge
This PM is true blue
And if you have no hair dryers
I'll point the sauce bottle at you

I mentioned to my cobber Forksy –
John Faulkner to you
I said strewth, Forksy matey
It's enough to make you spew
It really gets me goat up
I get cheesed off every day
And then I did forget whatever
I was going to say

So do not come the raw crustacean
Or you'll cop some lip
I'm flat out like a frill-neck
On me international trips
I'm boned up on the lingo
I can speak grouse Mandarin
But fair shake of the carpet snake
I'm dinkum Australian

I'm An Adelaide Man

WORDS: Greg Champion
TO THE TUNE OF: I'm a Honky Tonk Man

Stereotyping South Australians has never stopped amusing *The Coodabeens* in the thirty-six years I've been a part of it. This was from around the early Nineties.

I'm an Adelaide man
that's just what I am
I like to go to galleries
see some theatre when I can
I like to wear my kaftan
and drive a Kombi van
Because hey, hey, hey, I'm an Adelaide man

I'm an Adelaide guy
I went to Campbelltown High
We like our winery weekends
We go to Victor with our friends
We have a riesling with lunch
and a cheese dip to munch
Won't ya understand
I'm just an Adelaide man

I'm an Adelaide bloke
I'm into reggae and folk
We go to Thebarton Town Hall
We like to hang 'round Rundle Mall
We like to see the Crows play
and crack a chardonnay
Singin' hey, hey, hey we're all Adelaide persons

The Coodabeens Rode Into Tamworth

WORDS: Greg Champion

Sometime in the late nineties, *The Coodabeen Champions* went to Tamworth Festival to present their national show. Some *Coodabeens* had been rather merciless on the virtues of bush poetry—so a piece about the visit, in bush poetry style, seemed in order.

The cry went out around the land the Festival was on
From Dinky Creek to Bogan Hills from Yarck to Jigallong
The talk of Tamworth even reached the *Coodabeens* in Lithgow
Said Ian to Jeff, said Bill to Greg, by crikey, I think we'll go

They saddled up their horses and they journeyed 'cross the plains
O'er hill and dale—oh cut it out! They flew in on a plane
Strewth! they declared, we're finally here, this is gonna be so spesh
We're finally gonna get to see Lee Kernaghan in the flesh

They'd called the organisers saying we only have one rule
We'll only come if we can stay at the joint with the guitar-shaped pool
Gadzooks! they cried, there's more folks here than five Kentucky Derbies
If we play our cards right we might even meet Nick Erby

They headed straight for main street, they heard a mighty ruckus
The mighty, thunderous Peel Street roar of a hundred thousand buskers
They heard Bobbie McGee, Country Road's ten versions of Jambalaya
Help Me Make it Through The Night and a dozen Ring Of Fires

Stone the flamin' crows! they cried, I think we're havin' fun
If we could only meet Nick Erby our mission would be done
The Goodies and the Loco the Longyard and the Pub
They lapped up the Bush Poetry at North Tamworth Bowling Club

Beccy Adam Gina Troy one by one they met
But time was tight and still they hadn't found Nick Erby yet
They'd brought along their fold-up chairs they had a clear agenda
The all-day free entertainment in the Southgate Shopping Centre

Apart from that said Ian to Jeff, I fear I will be grumpy
If I do not get to meet my hero, Bruce McCumstie
Once introduced to Nick and Bruce, they stated glowingly
Country Music's ripper mate! and we LOVE bush poetry

Mathematics

Greg Champion [BMG publishing]

A bit of whimsy from the eighties.

One plus one is three
three plus three is four
four plus four is twenty-five
I'm tellin' you for sure
That's mathematics
that's how I get my kicks
I don't like wine or women give me
Good ole 'rithmetic

Three times three is eighteen
times four is twenty-two
mathematics works for me
and I'm convinced it can for you
I just love mathematics
it gets me every time
five plus five is twenty
eight plus eight is eighty-nine

If I had mathematics
I tell you what I'd do
I'd take my mathematics
and I'd share some of it with you
'Cos I just love my mathematics
mathematics is where it's at
one is one is one
two is two and that's a fact

If I had twenty dollars
I'd multiply by three
I'd add another hundred
think how rich I would be
That's good old mathematics
mathematics makes me smile
How 'bout you and me babe
get together do some maths for a while

Daintree

WORDS: Greg Champion [BMG publishing]

Triggered from a visit to the tiny town of Daintree, in FNQ, in the eighties.

There was a town called Daintree
and Daintree was its name
The locals all knew it as Daintree
but it was Daintree just the same

On the map it was known as Daintree
deep in the Daintree region it lay
Just near the Daintree tennis courts
smack bang on the Daintree highway

And all the people 'round Daintree
were in Daintree more or less
And why they called it Daintree
was anybody's guess

Everyone who came to Daintree
thought it was really good
And when asked if they thought they might come back one day
most of them usually said yes, they probably would

And all the people of Daintree
they loved their little town
And the fame and the legend of Daintree spread
for several miles around

It was a grouse little place old Daintree
and that's why it's such a shame
Every time I drive through Daintree
I can never remember its name

The Wrong Side Of Warrigal Road

WORDS: Greg Champion

Continuing a recurring theme, and a running gag, among my old friends.

You start out in St Kilda
and move to St Kilda East
then somehow you're in North Caulfield
but you're safe for a while there at least

You find yourself in Malvern East
and then Glen Iris too
before you know it you're in Ashburton
and Warrigal Road's looking at you

Warrigal Road's staring at me
staring at me, I'll be blowed
heaven help me if I ever have to move
to the wrong side of Warrigal Road

The Greatest Player To Ever Toss A Dart

Greg Champion

This began life as a poem, but I noticed later you could sing it to *All Among The Wool*. The noble art of darts is a source of never-ending amusement to me. Every time I come across it on a sports channel I chuckle at the obsession this 'sport' can generate. It was in a *Guardian* sports report that I saw the above title—undoubtedly with tongue in cheek—because the Brits are soooo good at that kind of irony! And Phil Taylor has such a low key name—and appearance also—for someone who's dubbed the best ever in this fine art. Furthermore, Phil was at the height of his powers when an unknown Aussie bricklayer, Simon Whitlock, seeded 98, got through to the final in a fairy tale, and *almost* defeated The Greatest Player to Ever Toss a Dart.

Now this here be the true tale of a giant of history
A Britisher so gifted he was dubbed a deity
A lad so skilled and talented in so revered an art
That millions loved The Greatest Player To Ever Toss A Dart

His given name was Philip, Phil Taylor his full name
And never in the Empire had one enjoyed such fame
To some it was a trifling thing a flighty, dreary game
But once Phil Taylor tossed a dart the sport was ne'er the same

Oh, they came down from The Highlands and across the windy moors
They rode in boats from Ireland, united in their cause
They hiked for miles from Dingley Dell, they flocked from Woodley Hart
To see The Greatest Player To Ever Toss A Dart

Then, from the far flung colonies a broad bricklaying type
Came forth to challenge Britain's best without a hint of hype
He turned up unannounced, with a mission in his heart
To devastate the Kingdom in the noble art of darts

His ranking it was ninety-eight a long way from the top
But through the early rounds they found his run could not be stopped
He took 'em on, he brushed 'em off, kept winning freakishly
Along the way he beat the seeds with rankings: two, and three

And while the Empire watched in awe, the Aussie Wizard found
He was to fight The Lord Of Darts to wrest the sacred crown
This weird Antipodean chased the ultimate conquest
And when the final dart was flicked our bold crusader's quest

Had failed but by a whisker, to upset the applecart
Snuffed out by The Greatest Player To Ever Toss A Dart

Oh they came down from The Highlands and across the windy moors
They rode in boats from Ireland, united in their cause
They hiked for miles from Dingley Dell, they flocked from Woodley Hart
To see The Greatest Player To Ever Toss A Dart

Someone's Moving Heavy Timber 'Round A Yard

WORDS: Greg Champion

Only now, decades later, do I see my love of Robert Frost's work reflected herein.

I heard a crack as I sat
indoors but idly listening
Then standing on the porch
as if on guard
the clatter of machinery
is out there somewhere
and someone's moving heavy timber 'round a yard

There's smoke through the valley
from a woodyard further up
it must be there
the noise is coming from
The Marysville winterscape
would otherwise be still
but for someone shifting timber 'round the mill

They're Building A Dairy

WORDS: Greg Champion

The dairy in question was at Carlisle River, in the Otways. Mid-eighties

They're building a dairy
They'd best make it strong
Tt's up from the old one
and just along
from the cowyard and back
from the house on the track

They're building a dairy
where the old one has stood
but this one's in brick
the former of wood
Timber crouched
in dusty respect
the patient builder
who dutifully wrecked it

And a new one is there
where men have stretched
to measure the ground
and beams have been fetched
and labourers found
to hasten the work
The sawmill pair
the brothers, the milker
all plodded there
and Dad's mechanic
with the ginger hair

Moving To South Caulfield

WORDS: Greg Champion

From 1983.

I'm moving to South Caulfield
it won't be as hectic as here
there'll be less visitors
I know it's a bit further out;
I guess I'll get used to it

I'll be moving to Caulfield soon
it should be fun;
We may not see as much
of each other but
I guess it's for the best

It'll be okay in Caulfield;
I reckon
be a bit more peaceful anyway
less traffic; not so much
shouting and fighting

I've never lived in Caulfield before;
particularly South Caulfield;
It should be good;
not as much action
Anyway I'm shifting this weekend
South Caulfield – here I come

The Things I'm Gonna Do Tomorrow

WORDS: Greg Champion

From 1982.

The things I'm gonna do tomorrow
I'm really gonna do 'em
From the moment I get up
I'm just gonna rip right through 'em
I'm gonna leave no doubt
but that they can be done
And by early late mid-morning
I'll have 'em on the run

Before I start my breakfast
I'll be making a call or two
and checking off my list
the most important things to do
By late mid afternoon
I'll be well on my way
to making it a really
successful little day

What's At The End Of Warrigal Road

WORDS: Greg Champion [BMG Publishing]

It became an in joke amongst friends that Warrigal road marked the edge of the known universe. As we grew from our twenties to thirties, our choice of house and home tended to move ever closer to the Warrigal Road line. Across that border, we alleged, you would drop off the edge of the world.

My own residential (rental) history in Melbourne followed a linear path. From Acland Street to off Balaclava Road to Alexandra Avenue Balaclava, to Caulfield North to East Malvern and *finally*, the first home purchase, two streets inside of the dreaded Warrigal Road Death Zone.

Where do the animals go when they die
Who made the clouds that roll in the sky
Who's gonna help me carry my load
And what's at the end of Warrigal Road

One end is Mentone so quiet and deep
Like some mythical monster in a log fast asleep
It wanders away somewhere down by the beach
And falls into the bay and way out of reach

But what of the other end that's what bothers me
Every time I drive by I try so hard to see
There's that crazy old house so shabby and cracked
One day I might never come back

From Warrigal road from Warrigal road
Warrigal road from Warrigal road

Where do the animals go when they die
Who made the clouds that roll in the sky
How can a tadpole turn into a toad
And what's at the end of Warrigal Road

Of Warrigal road of Warrigal road
Warrigal road of Warrigal road

That Keilor Beat

Greg Champion [BMG publishing]–Nigel Lawrence–Mark Ferrie

From 2017. Mark Ferrie [bassman for *The Models, Rockwizz* house band, several historic Peter Lillie line-ups including *The Leisuremasters*—and our current pub band] said to me on the phone: this one has the *Tequila* feel. Knowing his history with Peter Lillie, a treasured writer about all things to do with Melbourne, I joked: "It's got the *Keilor* feel"? After sharing this smile with my 27-year duo partner Gary Carruthers, who lives in East Keilor, I imagined a song about it. Old pal Nasty Nigel came up with the big *Keilor!* shout.

Way back behind them Keilor shops
You can hear that rhythm and it never stops
Down 'round the corner of Green Gully Road
That's where the happening people go
Floating up from the park and it sounds so sweet
That's where ya hear That Keilor Beat
Keilor!

Down 'round the flats off Keilor Park Drive
Saturday night this place is alive
see the bodies all shakin' in the evening heat
That's where ya hear That Keilor Beat
Keilor!

Let the traffic roll by on the old ring road
If you're out on the Calder it's go, man go
They're all whizzin' down to them big DFOs
When the only place to go is –
Keilor!

Just as it's gettin' on around near dark
The people all drift down to Brimbank Park
Oo baby, you're lookin' so sweet
Come and dance with me to That Keilor Beat

Makes you shake your hips, makes you tap your feet
Everybody movin' to the Keilor Beat

We All End Up In The Torrens

Greg Champion

My mother is 88 and for most of her life she's lived near the picturesque Morialta Reserve at the foot of the Adelaide Hills. She told me she came there to church picnic days in the forties, with crowds arriving in swarms by tram! She says that is the place for the final journey.

Speaking with Mum
about those who'd moved on
She told me of one
whose ashes were cast in the Torrens

And that her own choice
was the creek at Morialta
to which I ventured
Well you too will end up in the Torrens

We all end up in the Torrens
by one means or other
fair means or foul
physically or figuratively;
When the chickens have roosted
and the soul train's departed
and we've stopped having birthdays
and the horse has bolted
and the last ball's been bowled;
we all end up in the Torrens

if The Land of the Crow
is the one you call home
If Granite Island
and the Barr-Smith lawns,
If Popeyes and pie carts
shape the shadows of yesterday;
then whether you embrace her at Dernancourt
or behind the University
you may be sure it's your destiny
as sure as Coopers Sparkling Ale
shall forever, with sediment, be cloudy
When the final siren sounds
across Hectorville football ground;
we all end up in the Torrens

Leyland P76

WORDS: Greg Champion
TO THE TUNE OF: Universal Soldier

Way back in the early times, *The Coodabeens* would discuss memorable and dud cars of our youths. The Leyland P76 holds a special place in Aussie hearts, notorious for its unreliability and oddness. Listeners regaled us with P76 yarns and experiences, with some tales of alarming ineptitude in their factory construction. However, we did attend a P76 car rally, in Adelaide, and discovered that many people still adore their P76s.

Oh, P76 Leyland P76
you are the very pits and I dislike you
your ugliness is legendary your existence is a joke
you never ever should've been built at all

Oh, uglier much uglier than an old Toyota Crown
even more of a tank than a Charger
more horrible to contemplate than a panel van with beach scenes
with an engine like a sick 120Y

Just the very sight of you makes people wanna spew
you haven't got a friend in the world
you're a dud, you're a shocker, on a par with an Austin Tasman
and the folks who designed you should take a good hard look at themselves

Even less class than a four-cylinder Torana
nowhere near as interesting as a rusty Hillman Hunter
not even in the same carpark as a Kombi with the wheels off
you are the very terriblest car of all

Oh, P76 Leyland P76
you never ever should've been built at all

Slow Down To Eighty

Greg Champion [BMG Publishing]

Some very highly motivated people in Swanpool, near Benalla, were still helping farmers recover from the 2009 fires, in 2015. For the cause, I went to sing at the Swanpool Memorial Hall. Before going there one of the locals spoke with me on the phone, and while talking of the virtues and merits of Swanpool he said: "Not bad for a town that you only have to slow down to eighty for".

The town's pride and joy is the cinema
A memorial hall, original cinema
The store has been recently done up
It does postal and papers, petrol and liquor
We've got a Cemetery Trust and a Primary School
and our CWA is proud and strong

The creeks are still flowing, the trees are still growing
Tell ya what, that's not bad goin'
for a town that you only have to slow down to eighty for

We just lost our footy and netball sides
and there's still some grievin' and disbelievin'
They asked us to merge, we're not havin' it
but we're holding meetings, we're still not beaten
and our Uniting Church has been open for business
continuously since 1910

The creeks are still flowing, the trees are still growing
All in all, that's not bad goin'
for a town that you only have to slow down to eighty for

We're still fighting back from the bushfires
Six years later, still out there fencing
Still raising money for fencing gear
We need a thirty-six thousand dollar tractor
It's amazing what a bit of fencing can do
to put a smile on a battling farmer's face

The creeks are still flowing, the trees are still growing
Tell ya what, that's not bad goin'
for a town that you only have to slow down to 80 for

A town that you only have to slow down to 80 for

Never Turn Right At Burke Road Malvern

Greg Champion [BMG Publishing]

From 1986. This has been an enduring one, oft requested. I was living in a semi-detached rental in East Malvern and the great Burke Road-Malvern Road Bongo intersection was on the route into town. Waiting impatiently as usual on a looong red light there, to turn right from Malvern into Burke, I made a mental note to myself which became the title above. Then came the thought: that sounds like a silly song…

You can drive me down to Carlton
to pick up some stuff
You can hang around in Oakleigh
just waiting for a bus
to take you down to Moorabbin
watch them old Saint boys play
but don't you ever turn right at Burke Road Malvern
'cos you'll be there all day

I knew a man called Stanley
tough kinda guy
He'd fought in both the wars you know
I'd never seen him cry
Last I saw of old Stanley
he'd gone to cut his hair
He was turning right at Burke Road Malvern
And he's probably still there

Old Jean lived at Ashwood
with old Uncle Ern
He went out to do the shopping one day
And never returned
Many long years later when they'd
given him up for dead
They found his body in the car at Burke Rd Malvern
And the lights were still red

I Do Like To Be In Abu Dhabi

Greg Champion [BMG publishing]

I can't recall if I got into Noel Coward's work before or after this—in 2012—but I do see links to Noel's style here.

I like to take tea in Dharamsala
I only drink coffee in Kampala
When in the high plains of Argentina
I give concerts on my concertina
I own hotels in Addis Ababa
In Dhaka I have my favourite barber
I visit Japan to buy wasabi
But I do like to be in Abu Dhabi

At Epsom I watch the Epsom Derby
In Australia I love a barbie
In Africa I avoid Mugabe
But I do like to be in Abu Dhabi

I've seen the delights of Suriname
In Tashkent I have a private army
Whenever I'm stopped in Kiribati
The King there, he throws a lavish party
I do highly recommend Botswana
Especially the swimming with piranha
Of the many charms of French Guyana
You will not find a finer banana

At Epsom I watch the Epsom Derby
In Australia I love a barbie
In Africa I avoid Mugabe
But I do like to be in Abu Dhabi

I'm known to relax in Rawalpindi
In Riyadh the weather is too windy
While dining in Kota Kinabalu
An Englishman walked by and said "hallu"
I like dining out when in Djibouti
The fruit in Djibouti tastes so fruity
I just love the summers in Lesotho
You must come, so you can take my photo

My stylist lives in Burkina Faso
When there we discuss only Picasso
Should you come to Tierra Del Fuego
Please call me, I'll be in Pago Pago

At Epsom I watch the Epsom Derby
In Australia I love a barbie
In Africa I avoid Mugabe
But I do like to be in Abu Dhabi

Twenty-First At The Football Club

Greg Champion [BMG publishing]

It was a fella who can really make you laugh—long-time collaborator Colin Buchanan—who offered the observation that every time you play up bush, your audience is wiped out by a function at the sports club, or—something else.

We wander high we ramble low
to bring to town our humble show
To all points on the map we go
to far-flung spots we hardly know
And then the publican declares
he's sorry there were so few there
but the reason that your show was snubbed
is a twenty-first at the football club

The agent calls, you've got a gig
it sounds like this one could be big
She says it's up the Woop Woop Road
We pack the truck and off we go
and afterwards we meet the boss
who tells us that our timing's off
It's usually packed, but here's the rub
it's eight-ball night at the bottom pub

How often have you heard it said
you should have come last week instead
They're a funny mob round here, no doubt
you put things on, they won't come out

They thought they'd chuck a Festival
and happily we got the call
A big PA, stage and lights
an outdoor job, a Saturday night
We get there and the crowd looks poor
and then the fella on the door
says you haven't got a hope in hell
It's bingo night at the RSL

And you would've missed out anyway
There's a hen's night at Shirl's Cafe

So wandering minstrels you've been urged
beware the poor musician's scourge
It's a hiding to nothing, playing in pubs
against a twenty-first at the football club

And the top pub's packed out anyway
they got jelly-wrestling in lingerie

Upper Kumbuckna

Greg Champion [BMG Publishing]

An Aussie town with the name of Buckenyama just tickled me. I tell people before I sing this that these two remote towns are out there on the border of New South Wales, South Australia—and—Western Australia.

She was from Upper Kumbuckna
he from Buckenyama
They met beneath the town hall lights
at a dance in Unda Gumbunga
She was the local netball star
he a long-legged farmer
When the Upper Kumbuckna belle she fell
for the Buckenyama charmer

She was a drop-dead gorgeous sort
a rolled gold perfect ten
And she fancied the Buckenyama bloke
from the minute he walked in
She locked her eyes upon him
he arksed her for a dance
And so began the Upper Kumbuckna-Buckenyama romance

He was awful nervous
and she was kinda coy
when the Upper Kumbuckna beauty fell
for the lucky Buckenyama boy

At a chapel in Uptagundooka
the lovestruck couple were wed
The party ran till daylight in
the Unda Gumbunga woolshed
He had a grin from ear to ear
she looked queen of the world
When the Buckenyama farmer wed the Upper Kumbuckna girl

From Bunjalunga and Porepunkah
from parts of Congupna they came
From Dumbuganuckya and Rubadubduckya
and places too lengthy to name
And soon there were three little rug rats
In no time at all there were seven
For the Upper Kumbuckna-Buckenyama marriage made in heaven

The stars shone down upon them
the heavens danced with joy
when the Upper Kumbuckna beauty wed
the lucky Buckenyama boy

William The Wonderboy Of Willabangadoo

Greg Champion [BMG publishing]

If you can be charged with being too silly with place names, lock me up now.

Way up the Inkajinky in the land of Warrumbidgee
In the territory known as Wonkadingadoo
Near the Jimkumbingee River lived an interesting fella
William The Wonderboy of Willabangadoo

As a child he would wander 'round the hills of Winkadonga
And he'd paint all the scenery 'round Inkadongaroo
And his mother would say, where ya been all day
And he'd say, up to Nillumbunka, down to Winkywoo

Way up the Inkajinky near the Jinkumbingee River
Between Inkadonga and Wonkadingadoo
Past Oodnabalabie and Boolabillagabie lived
William The Wonderboy of Willabangadoo

One day while a-walking from Wonkaroo to Willabri
He came upon a wombat near Willawonkydoo
A baby wombat who'd lost his family
He cried, and he asked young Willy what to do

So William The Wonderboy scooped the baby wombat up
And knocked on the door of every wombat home
Until young Willy finally found the wombat's family
Down a dark hollow up the Wonkadinka Road

Way up the Inkajinky near the Jinkumbingee River
Between Inkadonga and Wonkadingadoo
Past Oodnabalabie and Boolabillagabie lived
William The Wonderboy of Willabangadoo

So it came to pass that William The Wonderboy
And the baby wombat became close pals
And they sat together by the Jimkumbingee River
And happily whiled away hours and hours

Way up the Inkajinky near the Jinkumbingee River
Between Inkadonga and Wonkadingadoo
Past Oodnabalabie and Boolabillagabie lived
William The Wonderboy of Willabangadoo

Like A Book On A Shelf

WORDS: Greg Champion–Nigel Lawrence
TO THE TUNE OF: Bird on a wire

Nigel started the whole ditty thing rolling back in Adelaide in 1977. He and I are still finding fresh ones; this is more recent. Nigel pointed out that some of the similes in Leonard Cohen's (immortal) *Bird On A Wire* were dubious, e.g. *like a fish on a hook*. That is how this piece began.

Like a frog in a lake
Like the icing on an old piece of cake
I have tried in my way to be deep

Like a duck on a pond
Like a song that goes on and on
I can make stuff up like that all day

Like a pig in a sty
Like a pupil in an eye
Like a white fluffy cloud in the sky

And If I have ever disappointed you
well don't worry, I've let others down too
And if I have ever sung out of key
that's okay, it sounded fine to me

Like a book on a shelf
like something that's like something else
I have looked for connections between things

Like a knob on a door
Like a drunk passed out on the floor
I have forgotten where this was going

Real Estate Agents Are People Too

Greg Champion [BMG Publishing]

Going back a few years I received a message—directed to our radio show—requesting a copy of this song from two real estate agents who wanted to use it as part of their wedding celebrations. Happily obliged.

I used to think they were all a bit shonky
Thought they were taking me for a donkey
Given to making wild assertions
Down the food chain with used car salespersons

But they're really no different from me and you
Real estate agents are people too

They all have families to feed
They laugh, they cry, they love, they bleed
Some are nearly normal and quite unassuming
Some turn out to be surprisingly human

Yes I've got a little secret and I'll share it with you
Real estate agents are people too

If they tell you it's oozing with charm and style
just turn away and knowingly smile
If their sales pitch sounds shallow and silly
remember they're trained to gild the lily

They're just doing the job God gave 'em to do
Real estate agents are people too

They're into creative exaggeration
A shed is self-contained guest accommodation
There's no such thing as a dud property
Just a gilt-edged golden opportunity

And if it's falling apart at the seams
That's just a canvas on which to paint your dreams
And if you see the words "rustic charm"
That's industry code for uninhabitable barn

Yes I've got a little secret and I'll share it with you
Real estate agents are people too

So I've overcome my prejudice and bias
that Real Estate agents were all shonks and liars
So next time you need a new place to live
just give 'em a go, they got a lot to give

Yes they're really no different from me and you
Real estate agents are people too

What Are Youse On About Young Shazza

WORDS: Greg Champion–John Ogge–Jane Harris
TO THE TUNE OF: Where do you go to my lovely

I reckon it was Billy Baxter, during a *Coodabeens* Sunday night radio program, who wondered aloud what an Aussie version of the above tune would sound like.

You talk like Cheryl of Ipswich
And your words are so much hot air
Your clothes are Miss Myer and Kmart
And there's dark roots in your blonde hair, yes there are

You live in a one bedroom granny flat
'Round the corner from the bus stop
Where you keep your buckets of make-up
that you put on to go up the shop, yes you do

But what are youse on about, young Shazza
With your bourbon and coke and your fags
What's going on in that head of yours
You're a real little mystery bag, yes you are

I've seen all the street signs and milk crates
That you nicked from the streets 'round Geelong
And the trolley you stole from the Bi-Lo
That you hang out your washing upon, yes you do

The Others

You're legendary on Karaoke nights
You know all the best Kylie songs
You hog the microphone and you show off
But you sometimes get the words wrong, yes you do

When the snow falls you're found in Ballarat
With some blokes that you've only just met
And you slurp on your UDL vodka
But you never smoke your own cigarettes, no you don't (you smoke mine)

I've seen you at the 7-Eleven
Faggin' with your friends in your car
I know the mob you hang round with
And what a bunch of shockers they are, yes they are (they're my friends)

They say that when you get married
It'll be some rich bloke from Toorak
But I know the suburb you came from
I've seen you in tracky dacks!

This Was My Town

Greg Champion [BMG publishing]

We regularly stayed in Marysville holiday accommodation—maybe two dozen times. The last stay was two weeks before the town was lost to bushfire. Like many we were in love with Marysville. We had considered getting our own place there. Not just a pretty town—possibly Victoria's prettiest. When I heard my dear town was gone—as were 34 of its residents—I wanted to give her a song. Long may she live on. They gave this song a gong at the Victorian Country Awards.

This was my town
that was the primary school
there, the Swimming Pool
See them now

This was my town
that was the take-away
there, the new café
Look at them now

This is the church
at least, it was before
There, the General Store
See them now

And still somehow
they're sayin' that this town can –
can be rebuilt again
God help this town

It took my town
Took the patisserie
Strangely the bakery
did not go down

A park and a lake
A favourite playground
Come all, from all around
Rebuild this town

This is the church
At least, it was before
There, the General Store
See them now

This was my town
That was the primary school
There, the Swimming Pool
God help this town

It's Only August (But It Will Soon Be September)

Greg Champion [BMG publishing]

A pet topic: surviving winter.

It's only August but it will soon be September
It's coming inevitably
'cos where August goes September must follow
it's a time-honoured certainty

As good as the springtime can sometimes be
'round here they all agree
the rich mellow heady mid-Autumn sun
is this region's specialty

The glow of the days from mid-March to May
they say are the best of the year
and from mid-May on, the long cool nights come
and the crisp dewy mornings appear

We start to draw inwards and shelter indoors
when the shadow of June doth befall
And we can do little but wait by the fire
when the depths of July come to call

But early in August, almost unnoticed
something is silently stirring
And though little changes still we divine
the buds and the shoots are returning

It's only August but it will soon be September
but not soon enough for me
I'm just marking time until my sublime
glorious January

sweet joy-filled January

Three Crows

Greg Champion [BMG Publishing]

It seems that *The Three Ravens* is an English folk ballad from 1611. I thought I should shift the notion to Victoria's Western District. It was triggered by seeing three crows sitting together on a fence on a dirt track near Logan's Beach, Warrnambool—a whale watching spot. From my first album in 1990, in the last days of vinyl records.

Three crows sat on a barbed-wire fence
In Hampden Shire where the weeds are dense
Two lady crows and one fine gent
In a paddock at Derrinallum

Said one crow to the other crows
Tell me crows now do you know
She said tell me where do you suppose
Where, where, where is the feeding good?

Said another crow to the very first crow
Yes I know where I would go
She said yes, yes, yes I know
Where, where, where the feeding is good

Said the other two crows pray tell us where
That we might dine on the finest fare
Pray tell that we might all be there
Where, where, where is the feeding good?

And they gazed across the field
And this is what the first crow revealed

In Camperdown the worms are big
They lay on the ground you don't have to dig
You ask 'em nice they'll put on a jig
Down, down, down in Camperdown

Said the other crow, well I think I know
Where I would most enjoy to go
The worms down there are big as your nose
Down, down, down in Allansford town

And the two crows turned their heads
And this is what the third crow said

In Hamilton town the worms are good
They'd wave a flag for you if they could
They slip down the throat like good worms should
Down, down, down in Hamilton town

Three crows sat on a rusty gate
And talked about the food they ate
And made each other salivate
And rambled till the day was late
In a paddock at Derrinallum